# Luck Times Two

Sandra Wilson

The Luck Times Two book cover was designed by Sedona Wilson, based on an original painting (also by Sedona Wilson). Koi fish were chosen as the central image because they represent luck in Chinese culture.

Published in the United States of America by Eloise Anthony Publishing House

ISBN: 978-1-7350631-0-2

Disclaimer: This memoir portrays the events, places, conversations, and names to the best of my recollection and that of my daughter, Sierra. Some names have been changed. It is based on our memories and may not represent exact occurrences, and in places was embellished for the benefit of storyline.

# Acknowledgements

This book was a labor of love and while it was many years in the making, I am proud of this accomplishment. None of it would have been possible without the support of my husband of 34 years, Paul. He understood my desire to write this book and was willing to put our parental joys and struggles on display for the whole world to see. He is the love of my life and always supports my need to constantly push myself. To my kids, Sedona and PJ, for being a critical part of the story and for the beautiful examples of love that I used in my tale. I love you both so much. Thank you, Sedona, for creating the beautiful cover, which so perfectly reflects the luck we've had on our adoption journey.

To my charming daughter, Sierra, for bringing such happiness and love into our lives. You are amazing. Your assistance with the narrative was invaluable. The stories you recalled from China broke my heart all over again, and brought the memoir to life.

To Andree Cohen, my dear friend, for providing early encouragement and constructive critiques as I first began writing the manuscript. You've been a constant in my life for over 33 years, and a treasured friend. You're insightful, silly, and wise, and I love that I can always count on you for a much-needed laugh.

Brian Hushek, I've known you since I was a toddler and am blessed to have you in my life. You're always there when I need you. You're our travel buddy, de-facto uncle, co-worker, confidant, and the most dependable person I know.

To Gary Whorton, Dale Curtis, and Adele Baudelaire, who are the most supportive and marvelous friends. Your encouragement with the book and with life has been an inspiration to me. I am so blessed to know you, to vacation with you, and to share our special moments in life. You are part of our family forever.

Thank you to Cari Gerchick, my inspirational coach, adviser, and amazing friend who died in May 2019. You believed in my story and my family, and constantly inquired about my progress with the manuscript. Luck was on my side when I met you and I will miss you forever.

To my whole family, but most especially, Mom, Bob, Sheree, Kelsee, Joe, Barbara, and Ron. I love you and thank you for accepting us all as we were forming this unusual international clan. I couldn't have asked for a more caring, understanding, or loving support group. You are all remarkable people.

Thank you to my editing and publishing team. I couldn't have completed this book without Jane Ryder, my editor. She was a patient teacher, a cheerleader, a counselor, and a friend. She taught me that writing is an adventure, filled with difficulty and bliss. The road has potholes as your skills expand, there are collisions with your ego, and hazards come at you like a deer on the roadway. You must refine your abilities and be resilient as you grow. Thank you, also to John Peterson, for introducing me to Jane and for encouragement and writing advice throughout the process. And finally, my thanks to Colleen Sheehan for creating a beautiful book interior. I couldn't have asked for a more appealing design.

# Prologue: An Orphanage in Northern China

Fu Shuang only remembered certain events from her childhood. She knew that she didn't have parents or a biological family, but she felt that she belonged where she was, at her orphanage in Benxi. The orphanage was small, but comfortable. It was a place that she called home and meant it. The caretakers and workers were good to her and she loved the other orphans.

Her home was part of a larger institution, the Benxi Social Welfare Institute, which included administrative offices and housing for elderly and disabled adults as well as the orphans. It was surprisingly picturesque, with a pond across the street, terra-cotta tile pathways, and a playground that she and the other children liked to visit. The playground, which was covered in thick grass, had a teeter-totter, monkey bars, and a curvy slide. If the children fell, the bushy grass cushioned their tumble. The emerald-green mountains behind the institution were pure beauty and the weather was cool and crisp most of the year. The section of the institute that included the office and the adults was tan with a red-tiled roof; the building that housed the orphans was scarlet red and was located to the right of the larger administrative building. It was a place of nurturing and it had positive energy that touched the children and the adults. Fu Shuang felt fortunate to be living at the orphanage with good people who cared for her. She was at peace.

Fu Shuang didn't know her birth parents or any family members. An elderly lady had dropped her off at the doors of the orphanage when she was a newborn. Caregivers at the orphanage told Fu Shuang that the woman found her in a box in the middle of the street and brought her to the institute. Fu Shuang liked to think of the old woman as her grandmother, or *Nai Nai*. Whether she was truly a relation or not, Fu Shuang would never know.

Nai Nai was a constant in Fu Shuang's early life. She visited the orphanage often to hold baby Fu Shuang, feed her bottles, and spend time with her. The woman was kind and gentle with Fu Shuang. But one day, when Fu Shuang was a toddler, the woman just stopped visiting. When Fu Shuang was older, the orphanage workers told her the story of the woman who had found her. Fu Shuang didn't remember the old woman and asked why her Nai Nai had stopped visiting. The caretakers didn't know the answer. *Perhaps my Nai Nai died*, she thought.

Years later, Fu Shuang met an orphanage administrator who took a liking to her sunny personality. Even after he left employment at the orphanage, he returned to visit Fu Shuang, and she thought of him as her uncle, or *Shu Shu*. He brought Fu Shuang presents and gave her money to spend, and once he even took her out to eat at a restaurant, which was a huge treat. He was a constant comfort and he made her feel like there was someone who valued her specifically. But when she was ten, he also disappeared from her life.

The loss of these family replacements – abrupt and without explanation – was always a great blow to Fu Shuang, and she wondered if she had done something that caused them to go away. Like most people, she wanted to be special and to have someone dependable who cared for her. She wanted to *matter* to someone. Occasionally, the dejection and isolation would settle on her like a dark cloud hangs on a mountain before a storm. But Fu Shuang was naturally cheerful, so such times were always fleeting: the storm clouds would lift, and the sunshine would reappear as her inner joy bubbled up once more.

Despite the periodic bouts of loneliness, Fu Shuang's early years were pleasant, though poor. The orphanage was small and there were fewer than twenty orphans who shared their home with the elderly, and mentally and physically disabled adults. Money and food were tight, and the institution's residents were often left without necessities.

The adults and children were housed on separate floors, but Fu Shuang loved to talk with everyone and so would find her way to all the residents, no matter what floor they were on. She was greeted warmly wherever she went, especially by the elderly, who were always buoyed by her sweet nature and high spirits. Later, when the new orphanage was built, the adults were sent to another building. Fu Shuang still visited them, but it was much more difficult, and she missed them. Sometimes extended family members would pick up abandoned children, and the infants and toddlers were frequently adopted. All this meant a continual sense of loss to Fu Shuang.

Fu Shuang was friends with all the children at the orphanage because she was gregarious and kind. But Fu Shuang was a tomboy and she enjoyed being rambunctious with the boys. While she liked the girls, she rarely played with them. She thought their games were boring and she was much more interested in physical activities. Her best friend was a boy named Fu Lu. Fu Lu and Fu Shuang were inseparable, like brother and sister. The caretakers even dressed them in similar clothes: Fu Shuang's favorite shirt was a white sailor-like hoodie, while Fu Lu had a navy hoodie. Both had identical white-and-navy striped trim and sleeves. The two children ran, jumped, and played outside in the surrounding area whenever they were allowed, getting into mischief and generally being kids. Fu Shuang and Fu Lu were a team, and Fu Lu was always there for his "sister," even as the adults and the younger children came and went.

The orphanage administrators spent a lot of time soliciting donations, and had regular visitors and donors who brought clothes, food, and money to help improve living conditions in the facility. Once a month, Fu Shuang and Fu Lu would put on a show for the guests. These performances were meant to illustrate that the children at the center were happy and well cared for, which might bring in more donations. Both Fu Shuang and Fu Lu loved to perform, and it was a pleasure for everyone to see them on stage. They danced, sang traditional folk songs and current hits, and just generally entertained the visitors. After the show, the two mingled with the guests. As Fu Shuang floated about the room, she told the adults what a wonderful home the orphanage was, and Fu Lu talked about how all the kids and staff were like family. The cheerful, smiling kids helped the guests open their wallets; it was an effective fund-raising technique that the orphanage came to depend on.

Of course, not every day at the orphanage was joyful. In fact, many days the children were sad and lonely, and felt their poverty keenly. Life was difficult and unpredictable, and despite her young age, Fu Shuang was intimately familiar with hunger, illness, and death.

One morning she found a baby boy outside the door of the orphanage. He was very thin and appeared to be sick. She rushed him to the nursery and watched as the caretakers examined, fed, washed, and dressed him. The next day, when she went to nursery to feed the babies (the older children were largely responsible for the care of the younger ones), she picked up the infant she had found the day before. He wasn't moving. He was cold and pale, and his eyes wouldn't open. He was so fragile and weightless in her arms, like she was carrying a cotton ball. She took him to the caregiver to ask what was wrong with him and was told he had died during the night. Death was common in the orphanage, but that didn't mean she was used to it, and Fu Shuang was heartbroken. A beautiful, innocent child had lost his life. Fu Shuang didn't understand why the world was so cruel and she knew that this fate could've happened to her when she was a baby. She wondered – not for the first time, or the last – why some children lived, and others left the earth so soon.

Hunger was a daily component of life for Fu Shuang and her friends. The children were fed three times a day, but the meals were meager and didn't begin to fill their small bellies. If they were still hungry after a meal, it was unfortunate, but second helpings were out of the question. There were simply too many orphans and not enough food.

But kids are resourceful, and Fu Shuang was no exception. She offered to help in the kitchen after dinner, cleaning tables, washing dishes, and putting food away, because she received additional rations from the cook. When she wasn't working there, Fu Shuang and her friends simply stole from the kitchen when they were exceptionally hungry. The chef seemed to like Fu Shuang, so whether this thievery went unnoticed or the woman turned a blind eye, the girl and her friends were never punished and were occasionally able to supplement their sparse rations.

At an early age the older orphans were required to help with the babies. Feeding and changing the diapers of infants was routine. Fu Shuang was so hungry one day that she drank a bottle of milk that had been made for an infant when she found the baby sleeping. She was ashamed of her action, but her instinct for survival was strong.

One solution to the hunger pangs came on a day when Fu Shuang, Fu Lu, and their friend Sheng were out scavenging in the mountains surrounding the orphanage. The area was beautiful, with lush grass, stately ginkgo and pine trees, and steep hills dotted with snow-white rhododendron bushes and wild pink peonies. The kids climbed up into the mountains and came upon a Buddhist temple – a black pagoda-style building with red columns. They didn't know anything about Buddha except that they needed to be reverent and honor him at this spiritual site.

"I think we should investigate," Fu Lu said. "This looks like a place that might have useful stuff."

"We need to be careful and respectful," said Sheng.

"I know we're going to find something we can use," Fu Shuang said. "I can feel it in my very soul. I think we're supposed to be here."

They went into the temple and found fresh water, oranges, apples, and peaches that worshippers had left for Buddha. The children eyed this bounty hungrily.

"It's wrong to steal," Sheng said. "We need to leave now. I hear someone coming." When they listened, they heard distant footsteps making a soft, consistent drumming on the pavement.

"I'm too hungry to leave without food," Fu Lu said. "I'm going to take an apple."

"Sheng, Buddha wouldn't want us to be hungry," Fu Shuang said. "He wouldn't be mad that we took a little of his food. It would make him happy to make us happy. I'm taking an orange. Here, you take a peach."

Just then, a monk appeared in the distance, striding quickly up the path to the temple. He was silent but his step was determined, and his face was stern. The children took the fruit and immediately began to run.

"Go, go, go and don't look back!" Fu Lu said.

They ran down the hill and when they did look back, they saw the monk, who smiled and waved at them, not in the least upset. They let out a collective sigh, knowing they not only weren't in trouble but had the monk's blessing.

From then on, whenever they were outside running and playing in the hills surrounding the orphanage, they would visit Buddha and take a small amount of food. Not only did these snacks ease their own persistent emptiness, but sometimes they'd bring the food back for the smaller children at the orphanage. Fu Shuang always gave thanks to Buddha for providing food for her and her friends. "Buddha is definitely someone we need to know and respect. He is great and kind," she said. Each time they visited, they made a tradition of kneeling, hands in the prayer position, and giving him their petitions and gratitude.

—

Despite the constant hunger and occasional sadness, Fu Shuang was comfortable and content at the orphanage. She could play with her friends and visit with adults, and the staff was generally kind.

Then she turned eight.

When children reached that age, they were required to go away to a boarding school with other older orphans, so Fu Shuang and her friends left the only home they'd known and headed to boarding school. Ten grade-school children slept in a dormitory room with one high school or college student bunking with them as their room monitor. The school operated seven days and six nights per week. The kids were given one night off per week to rest. Class was from 7:00 a.m. to 8:00 p.m. with an hour break for lunch, and another hour break for dinner. Oftentimes, the kids would be required to jog first thing in the morning, even when the weather was extremely hot or cold.

Fu Shuang had one main teacher who taught most of the day, but a different teacher for science and history. The academic day was long, tedious, and filled with challenging work. The last hour of every school day was spent in the classroom completing homework. The children were required to do this in the classroom and did not have the opportunity to do it in their dorms. This scholastic structure may have forced a concentration on learning, but it also meant little joy for the children. Daily, they found themselves exhausted from the mental and physical rigor of the routine.

The children were expected to wash their own clothes, linens, and towels. The orphanage provided their clothing and gave the boarding school a small stipend for each child. These funds were held in trust for the children in case of emergency, and very occasionally released to them for toiletries and snacks. A convenience store next door to the school was the only place outside the grounds the kids could venture.

Fu Shuang hated the boarding school. It made her feel hopeless and dull, so unlike her active and cheerful self. She didn't like the rigorous school schedule, the food, or many of the teachers and caretakers. Her free time and autonomy had been stripped from her and she felt her enthusiasm for life drain away, like water flowing down a sink. She still had Fu Lu and the other kids from the orphanage, but now they had little time for play or creativity.

The food was an especially big issue for Fu Shuang. Though it was more plentiful at the school than it had been at the orphanage, Fu Shuang couldn't bring herself to eat most of it because she had saw it being prepared. There were always butchered pigs laid out on the floor in the cafeteria, split in half and left to drain of blood, which flowed from the animals into the open gutters scattered throughout the room. The carcasses were covered with flies, and the smell of rotting flesh was putrid, the stench of death present at every meal. Fu Shuang just couldn't deal with the sights or smells of the room, and it left her without an appetite. She found herself eating rice and maybe some vegetables, but nothing else. Hunger again became a focus of her day, though now, because the food was so unappetizing, she didn't even try to think of ways to get more to eat, she simply learned to live with the omnipresent pain in her stomach. The attitude at the school was "eat or go hungry," so Fu Shuang chose to go hungry.

As a direct result of this lack of nourishment, Fu Shuang became sickly. She had been a healthy child at the orphanage, but once she started school, she was always unwell. Stomach problems, fevers, flu, and upper respiratory infections – her illnesses were diverse and persistent. Fu Shuang hated being sick. This vibrant and vital girl, who loved to jump, run, climb, and keep up with the boys, became despondent when she was ill, which only made her sicker. She became a frequent visitor at the nurse's office. Once, her health deteriorated to a point where she couldn't stand or walk to the clinic by herself and her friends had to carry her. While she always recovered, she never returned to her old active self, and these cycles of ill health continued the entire time she remained at the school.

The boarding school was not in a good area of the city, and the children often felt unsafe, particularly the girls. They had good reason. One night, when Fu Shuang was eleven, she and the other girls heard something outside and looked out of the window. They saw a man, who had climbed the fence that surrounded the school, standing in the courtyard. He couldn't get into their room because there were bars on the windows, but they could see him staring intently right at them. He knew they'd seen him, but he didn't move or look away, just continued to gaze fixedly at the girls with a strangely malignant expression. He appeared to be in his fifties, with shabby clothing, an unkempt beard, and messy hair, but it was his demeanor that truly unnerved the girls. He had an empty gaze and a look on his face they all felt was simply evil. One of Fu Shuang's roommates made motions to shoo him away, but he didn't move. Another of the girls was so terrified that she left the room to find the supervising student on the floor, who then told a young man at the front desk what was happening. He got a group of men together and they went out to remove the Peeping Tom from the campus. When the men got close, the intruder jumped back over the fence and ran away. Fu Shuang didn't get any sleep that night but dreamed of the wicked man, a dream that continued to haunt her for many nights to come.

—

The children spent ten months of each year at the boarding school, and those months were arduous for Fu Shuang, but she was able to endure because she knew she would return to the institution in Benxi, even though it would only be for two months. When she was lonely, sad, scared, or sick at school, she'd think of her orphanage family waiting for her in Benxi, and she could be brave and continue with her head up. The orphanage was where her heart dwelled. The orphanage was home.

## Chapter 1: The Surprise in Phoenix

### Sandi

It was a chilly day in January 2004 in a city known for its hellish heat. The wind was sharp, and the temperature was in the fifties, which is quite cold for desert dwellers. We had gone downtown to see our six-year-old daughter, Sedona, perform in her first dance recital, and she was about to take the stage. Sedona was nervous in her pink Chinese firecracker outfit, but she looked adorable. It was a celebration of Chinese New Year sponsored by the organization Families with Children from China. Little did I know that the day would hold so much more than a sweet children's performance and family celebration.

The event was being held at Heritage Square, a stunning step back into the nineteenth century, situated in the center of Downtown Phoenix. An old brick Queen Anne Victorian, Rosson House is the centerpiece of the park. It was built in 1895 and is one of the oldest buildings in the city. With its regal attic tower and ornate black fencing and trim, the house demands to be noticed. However, on this day, the focus was on little Chinese girls and boys running about the park, squealing with delight. Parents huddled around picnic tables talking about typical parenting issues like day care, music lessons, time-outs, and sibling rivalry. But they also talked about the unique children who had joined their homes, and the equally unique problems they sometimes faced. These were families formed through adoption – American parents who had or were in the process of adopting children from China.

Many were first-time parents, anxious and excited to have transported their children home in recent months. Others were old pros, having more than one child and several trips to China in their histories. The experienced parents were giving advice to young couples or single mothers and fathers who looked sad, worried, and removed from the action. These potential adoptive parents were often waiting to be matched with an orphan, or they might have been slightly further along in the process, delayed by the official approval to travel to China and pick up their kids. As I sat at a picnic table with my son, PJ, on my lap, I remembered that empty *waiting* feeling and said a silent prayer for the soon-to-be parents around me.

I also felt a trace of envy. These expectant parents might not have their children yet, but they had so much to look forward to. There are few events as life changing as traveling to a foreign country to meet and bring home a child. I needed to add a little girl or boy to our family, but I wasn't going to have the opportunity and it made me melancholy. My mood was seeping into the energy at the table, so I tried to reengage with the people around me, but deep down I was still somber. *I want to adopt another child,* kept creeping into my mind. The words were written on my heart as surely as if a tattoo artist had inked them there.

My husband, Paul, and I had already adopted two wonderful children over the past five years. The elder, Sedona, was adopted from China when she was fourteen months old; Parker José, known as PJ, was adopted from Guatemala at ten months. Both were beautiful children, the loves of my life, but I had been trying to persuade Paul to adopt another. He thought we were too old for another baby. I had assured him that this time we would adopt a toddler or older, thinking that we could get a child between Sedona and PJ's age, maybe five years old. But Paul had always been intensely practical, and he reminded me that adopting more children was a cost we couldn't afford. We had already taken out a second mortgage on the house to pay for the last adoption, and of course that was just the beginning. Once each child was home there was day care, clothing, food, medical care ... the list went on and on. Later would come school and yet more costs, and these financial burdens would continue until the child was at least eighteen years old – probably much longer. So, in the end I agreed, but regret was taking over my mood on this brisk afternoon. I watched all the beautiful children in the park and dreamed of a larger family.

I finished eating and put PJ into his stroller. Sedona and Paul had already headed to the stage to get her ready for the dance recital. When I saw Sedona standing in line with the huge pink firecracker in her arms, my heart melted. She was so adorable with her two ponytails, in her fuchsia and turquoise Chinese outfit. I knew she would lose the jitters as soon as she began dancing. Sedona was a survivor in every sense. A beautiful child from the Shanghai region of China, she was striking, even at six years old, and as bright and determined as she was pretty.

A classic Chinese song began to play. I had heard this song a thousand times as Sedona practiced in class and at home. She danced magnificently, not missing a step. Paul and I took many pictures, both during and at the end of her performance, and afterward we watched the older children perform. As we sat enjoying the pageant, I saw an old friend approaching our row.

Sonja was one of my favorite people. She worked for Hand-in-Hand International Adoptions, the agency that had facilitated both PJ's and Sedona's adoptions. In fact, without Sonja, we wouldn't have been matched with PJ, since we were in the Filipino Program. But she had gotten to know us during Sedona's adoption, so she wisely called us about Little José from Guatemala, and it was love at first sight.

After having been through so much with her, we thought of her as a friend, and I expected today to be hugs and smiles, not business. But after we'd greeted each other warmly, she said she had something very important to discuss with me and asked me to come see her the next day at the adoption agency. With an air of urgency, she said, "It really can't wait, and I don't want to talk about it here. Please come to the office tomorrow."

She was being so mysterious my imagination immediately went into overdrive and I began to envision possible issues with my children's paperwork. Perhaps one of my kids' adoption papers was invalid or PJ's naturalization filing was not being processed as we had discussed? Whatever the problem, it must be serious. Sonja was a happy person, but today she looked worried and it put me on edge. I agreed to meet her the next day.

The rest of the Chinese New Year celebration was congenial as we caught up with other adoptive parents and friends, but I was still fighting alarm because of the ominous discussion with Sonja. On the way home, I told Paul about the conversation. As usual, he told me to stop worrying, but that wasn't easy for me. When it came to my kids, I was as protective as a mother bear, ready to attack anyone or anything threatening them. Since I didn't know what the threat was, though, I was reduced to useless fretting.

The next day, Monday, I took a long lunch from work and met Sonja at Hand-in-Hand. The agency was in a dingy brown business building and the office was filled with paperwork, pictures of children, and portraits of happy families. A beautiful assortment of diverse faces filled the frames with people who had benefited from international adoptions. It was clear that many of these folks did not share genetics, but all were glowing with love. This office represented joy and happiness for me. It was where I had first seen pictures of my daughter and son several years earlier. Today I was not so eager to enter, being sure Sonja had bad news for me.

When I arrived, she ushered me to her desk and quickly closed the door. Her office was filled with mounds of files and paperwork, attesting to the hours of dedicated work she put in every day; the walls were adorned with child-drawn pictures of families and beautiful thank-you cards, attesting to the gratitude and affection her clients felt for her. She peeked through the paper mountains and today her expression was one of hopeful anticipation, so I began to relax. I took several deep breaths and I found my presence, just as I would do if I were meditating or practicing yoga. Maybe this *wasn't* bad news. Hand-in-Hand was my happy place. I sat down and let her explain.

"I wanted to talk with you about considering another adoption, Sandi. I remember you telling me that you and Paul had discussed getting an older child. There is a girl from China I'm trying to place, and I want to talk with you about her. I've heard she's a treasure."

At that moment, my heart soared. This was an answer to my recurring prayer. I listened intently to everything she had to tell me. Even though Paul and I had agreed that another child would be ... impractical ... I was living in the present moment, the joy overflowing, and I wasn't about to let reality seep into the picture immediately. After all, it couldn't hurt just to discuss it with Sonja, could it?

She reached into her desk and pulled out a file. It was titled *Dang Fu Shuang*. The Chinese interpretation of the name *Fu Shuang* is "double luck," or "luck times two." My heart leaped again.

"The girl I'm trying to place is eleven years old. I've tried to get her adopted and have spoken to over a dozen families who are waiting for a match. I haven't been able to place her, and I only have a couple of weeks left to find her a home. She's on the 'special needs' list because of her age and a condition she was born with called clubbed feet. If I'm unsuccessful, her referral will be returned, and she won't be adoptable."

Sonja went on to explain that the orphanage that referred Dang Fu Shuang was new to international adoptions and that they'd sent the information because time was running out for her to be adopted. Once she turned twelve, they would stop trying to place her. Sonja handed me the file. It was filled with pictures of a child who appeared to be closer to eight than eleven. She had an innocent face, a large crooked smile, and mischievous eyes that shone with joy and confidence. She looked humorous in the posed pictures that were included; clearly, she was a ham and enjoyed the attention. I reviewed the material quickly and took the file from Sonja, but there was a lot to absorb and think about. I promised to call her the next day to discuss the idea in more detail.

—

Hand-in-Hand was located in the suburb of Mesa, and it was a forty-minute drive back to my office in Downtown Phoenix. As I drove, my mind raced. Paul would never agree. What if she completely disrupted our family serenity? Could she speak or read English? She'd need tutoring, which would be expensive. Her age would bring a whole host of complications. When I'd dreamed of adopting an older child, I was thinking between the ages three and six – not eleven! I just didn't think this would work. By the time I made it back to my office, I was so filled with anxiety my heart was no longer soaring – it was pounding.

I must admit that I didn't get much work done that afternoon. At the time, I was the deputy county manager and budget director for Maricopa County, the most populous county in Arizona at almost four million, and I had a lot to deal with. My schedule that afternoon was packed with meetings and paperwork, starting with a consultation on the budget submission from the Sheriff's Office. It was the largest budget we worked on each year, at approximately $141 million, and there were a lot of complications. The Sheriff's Office was requesting tens of millions of dollars in new equipment, building improvements, and personnel. This was big, important, expensive stuff, yet throughout the meeting my attention wandered to images of a sweet face with dancing dark eyes. Next on the agenda was a performance appraisal for an employee. She deserved my full attention but I'm afraid she got less on that day, as thoughts of Fu Shuang whirled in my head. I stared at my computer screen for the remainder of the afternoon, handling more mundane tasks so even though I was distracted, I could at least accomplish *something*, and I left on time, which was a rarity for me.

I had Fu Shuang's file in my briefcase and I couldn't wait to get home so I could begin to learn more about this eleven-year-old mystery girl. I hoped that after reading the information, my black-and-white image of Fu Shuang would magically become a full technicolor picture, which would somehow make it easier for me to know what to do. And while I wanted time alone with the file, I was more than a little nervous about sharing this development with Paul.

When I got home, I immediately opened the package and began to read. Fu Shuang was a straight "A" student, obedient, helpful, and happy. She was born with clubbed feet that were corrected when she was three or four years old. She had been abandoned, and the search for her birth parents was unsuccessful. There were pictures of her playing a guitar, talking on the phone, and posing in front of the orphanage. There were several pictures of her feet, showing that her disorder had been corrected. Her hair was cut unflatteringly short and her teeth were badly in need of braces, but her eyes were clear and happy. Her clothes were old and faded, like they had been handed down from child to child, but they looked clean.

Most striking was her joy. It radiated out of the photograph and her sweet nature seemed to penetrate the room. My desire to get to know her had worked a little too well; now it would be hard to let her go. I read through the papers and prayed. I prayed for wisdom, prayed that Paul would be open, and most importantly prayed that our decision would be in line with our family's destiny. Then I called for Paul.

"So, what did Sonja want today?" he asked.

I handed him the packet. "She wanted us to consider adopting this eleven-year-old girl from China. I didn't prompt this, I promise, she just saw us yesterday and thought we might be a good fit."

He opened the package and stared at the little girl in front of him. He wasn't protesting, and he wasn't talking; he was just gazing at the pictures. He sat down and began to leaf through the file. He looked at the pictures, he read and reread pages describing her history and personality, and finally after about twenty minutes, he spoke.

"She's adorable. She looks like a happy kid in need of a family." He looked up at me. "I think we should seriously consider this."

I was stunned. "What? Really?"

"I think we should seriously consider adopting her. It would be nice for Sedona and PJ to have an older sister. I know it might be a challenge, but we can handle it," he said with a smile.

Terror filled me when I heard these words. I had braced myself for complete rejection. I had expected to argue her case, but in the end lose the fight. I was speechless, confused, and petrified as I suddenly found I'd won without saying a word. I fell silent and prayed once more. Did I really want this? Would she be a good fit for the family? Could we handle the language barrier? Would she have behavior problems? Was she healthy after years in the institution? The list of potential difficulties was endless. Cold sweat began to run down my spine as I thought about Sedona and PJ, and how much her presence would change their lives.

So, I reversed course and began discussing all the challenges. I was spitting out the questions that were running through my head, like the news ticker that runs across the bottom of the television screen during a CNN broadcast.

In typical fashion, Paul cocked his head at my verbal assault and in a calm voice said, "I thought you wanted this?"

I took a deep breath and said, "I'm worried about how she might change the dynamic of our family. She's going to have a formed personality. She isn't going to speak English. She might not get along with Sedona and PJ. I'm so confused, and I'm scared." Panicked beyond recognition might have been the best description. I don't know what I looked like in that moment, but probably like a ghost: pale and petrified, with wild, empty eyes.

He took my hand and said, "Let's have a family meeting. We need to explain this to Sedona and PJ and get their take on it. We can do it after dinner, okay?"

I nodded and went to lie down. Usually when I got home from work I was excited to spend time with the kids and hear about their days. I liked to have them describe their day in one word – *happy*, *tired*, *bored*, et cetera. – because it gave me a good idea of what I could expect from them the rest of the evening. But today I needed time to think about our challenges and the difficult decision before us. I stayed in the bedroom and let the thoughts swirl around my head.

When Paul called me to dinner, the aroma of chicken and macaroni-and-cheese filled the air. The four of us sat at the table eating, and I could tell the kids sensed that something was amiss because they were hyperactive, chattering even more than usual. My kids had always been very receptive to the energy of a room, and these two had pegged the nervousness coming from Paul and me. Especially me, I think.

Paul and I had been married for thirteen years before we brought Sedona home. We were both quite set in our ways when we decided to adopt the first time, but the process – a journey like no other – reignited our marriage. It had happened with PJ, too; it was as if we'd drunk a potion that filled us with even more love for each other, as well as love for the new members of our family. But now we'd been married for nineteen years, and I wondered if bringing another, much older, child into the mix would have the same effect.

After dinner, we took the kids to the living room. We seldom used that space. In fact, for most of our married lives it had sat unfurnished, and we'd only made it usable when we'd been preparing for the home study prior to Sedona's adoption. Home studies are required for adoptive parents. The adoption agency visits the home to evaluate it for safety and comfort; it's part of the process of determining if a family is suitable.

We only used the living room for important family meetings, so the kids knew something was up. Sedona's eyes were bright, and she was sitting up very straight, ready to absorb whatever we were about to say. PJ, being so much younger, was restless and running around with his Buzz Lightyear action figure.

I jumped right in because I knew the kids were on edge, and I didn't want them to think they were in any kind of trouble.

"I talked with Miss Sonja today about the possibility of adopting another child. We want to tell you about her, and we want you think about it. Would you like an older sister?

We'll only adopt her if everyone agrees this is a good idea. We're a family, and it's as much your decision as ours."

"Older sister," Sedona said. "What do you mean?" There was alarm in her voice, and she looked at me as though I had cut her with a knife. Her eyes flickered to her father, and back to me.

I explained that the girl was eleven and was in China, waiting to be adopted. She had been at the orphanage her entire life and would like to come to America and be a part of a real family. I handed over the packet to Sedona and PJ and they began looking through the pictures.

PJ smiled as he pointed at Fu Shuang. "She looks nice," he said.

But Sedona's expression was grim, and she wasn't going to be distracted from her question. "You mean she's going to be the oldest? She's going to be *my* older sister, *PJ's* older sister?"

"Yes," I said calmly, knowing where this was going. "Her name is Dang Fu Shuang. It means luck times two."

Slowly and deliberately, Sedona began to shake her head. "No! I don't want an older sister. I want to be the oldest. I *am* the oldest."

Paul took over. "Sedona, honey, this might be her last chance to have a family. She's eleven and she needs to be placed soon, or she'll have to stay at an orphanage for the rest of her life."

"I'm sorry," Sedona said, "but I want to be the oldest. I don't need an older sister. *I* want to be PJ's older sister. His *only* older sister. I want to be the oldest kid in the family. I *am*, and I want it to stay that way."

At six, Sedona was certain of her place in the world. She was opinionated and determined. She was already running the household, from her perspective, and she and PJ had a close relationship where, clearly, she was in charge.

PJ was confused and distracted. I tried to engage him as well, but he was only three and I don't think he truly understood what was happening. At this point, he was mostly worried about Sedona's reaction, so he looked miserable. Sedona was not the kind of child who cried or threw a tantrum, she just spoke her mind. PJ took his cues from his older sister, and gloom descended on him like a shroud.

Paul and I talked about Dang Fu Shuang for a little while longer but closed out the discussion with, "We'll talk more about this tomorrow." We put the kids to bed, then went up to our bedroom and debated the issue a little longer without coming to any conclusions, and I went to sleep that night with dread. I had been leaning toward adopting this child, but after the discouraging reception we'd gotten from Sedona and PJ, it didn't feel like the right thing to do. Still, I couldn't stop thinking of Fu Shuang and picturing an hourglass with the sand almost drained. I dreamed of a little girl with short black hair and mischievous eyes.

—

The next day I decided to confide in my good friend, Andree. I'd met her years ago when I'd worked at American Express, and she had followed me to Maricopa County for a time. She was Sedona's godmother and was a wonderful sounding board whenever I had problems. Born and raised in New Orleans, she had a different perspective on life that I always admired. She was more adventurous than I was and enjoyed life fully. She loved her son Robbie, her sister Luise, food, and fun. She had moved around the country and had lived in New York, New Mexico, Louisiana, Arizona, and had recently moved back to New Orleans. Happiness surrounded her spirit and still does.

Over the phone, I told her about Dang Fu Shuang. She listened intently as I recounted my concerns, my hopes for a larger family, Paul's response, and Sedona's reaction. Then she began asking me questions about finances, family support, childcare, and our home and living arrangements. She brought up something I hadn't even thought of. We had a three-bedroom house and the rooms were all occupied. "Is Sedona going to share a room with Fu Shuang? Won't that make the situation even more strained?"

She had a point, and my heart began to sink as I thought, "*Even Andree thinks it would be a mistake.*"

Then she asked, "Isn't it true you've been praying for another child? Didn't the prayers involve an older child?"

I had to admit that I had prayed for just that.

"Well, when God sends you an answer, I think you should say yes."

I was blown away. As she often did, Andree had made everything clear.

We should adopt Dang Fu Shuang.

Yes, this clearly was an answer from above. Now the issue was convincing Sedona and hoping that she'd have a change of heart. I prayed for a heavenly intervention and then I released my desire into the universe. It was time to let go.

## Chapter 2:
# Meanwhile in Benxi

### Fu Shuang

Dang Fu Shuang lived at the Benxi Social Welfare Institute Number Two in a rural area of Liaoning Province, northeastern China. The province is in an area known as the Golden Triangle, so called because of its shape and its location near the Yellow Sea, bordering North Korea. The name *Liaoning* is made up of two Chinese characters: Liao, meaning *far* or *distant*, and Ning, meaning *peace* or *calm*, which aptly describes this area of China. *Liao* is also the name of the river that flows through the entire province.

The city of Benxi has a population of 1.7 million and is highly industrialized, known for its coal mining and steel production, which creates a great deal of pollution in the otherwise picturesque area. Fu Shuang's orphanage was a three-story building, comfortable and clean, set in a rural area of the Liaoning Province. The road to the orphanage was badly maintained dirt, making access difficult. The topography was lush, scattered with farms growing crops of all kinds, including medicinal herbs like ginseng, and fruit such as apples, peaches, and plums. Cornfields dotted the landscape throughout the road from Shenyang, and during harvest time, the tall stalks swayed in the breeze like waves of green. Bicycles with makeshift trailers hauling live chickens were part of the daily routine. The rural area also featured many cattle ranches, and elderly men and women were frequently seen leading cows down the road. It was a beautiful place to grow up: peaceful and serene.

At the orphanage, the younger children were required to stay indoors and were not allowed to roam freely outside, but the older kids were permitted to use the playground across the street, and even wander the countryside. Their outdoor adventures kept the kids in good spirits. Fu Shuang was active and energetic, running around with the boys, climbing mountains, investigating the surrounding area, and getting into trouble. She didn't like girlie activities that happened inside the orphanage, and chose to spend her days outside whenever possible.

New children arrived at the orphanage every day. When younger kids came, Fu Shuang and the older kids were asked to give up their beds and sleep on the floor to make room, a custom accepted as normal by all the children.

Once, four siblings arrived together. The children were despondent, like hollow human forms, walking around the corridors without emotions. Their eyes were blank, and they did not want to interact with the other children. The caretakers told the older kids that these poor orphans came to the institute after their parents committed suicide in front of them. The sibling group was sent to live across the road at the home of a deaf adult who was being cared for by the institute.

Fu Shuang, an empathetic child, thought about the horror these poor orphans had suffered. Having no memory of her own parents, she had never missed them, yet she could imagine the intense hurt of these four siblings. She visited them often, trying to brighten their lives with stories, jokes, and games, and they became friends. One of the boys, Sheng, was her age, and they became especially close.

Life for all the orphans was far from comfortable. Their clothes were hand-me-downs many times over; they slept together in a dormitory room, lucky to have a bed; food was sparse. Many of them had never experienced life outside the walls of the orphanage, so they accepted this lack of comfort as normal and were able to remain joyful.

Fu Shuang had seen other children leave the orphanage. Babies and toddlers were adopted regularly, and it was like a revolving door as the infants were shuttled in and out of the home. Fu Shuang was always happy for the children who received families of their own, and she never questioned why it didn't happen for her. Having been at the orphanage her whole life, she just didn't think about it much. She had friends, shelter, and food, even if it was never enough.

She was content and her life was complete, so when she was told she was going to be presented for adoption, she wasn't sure it was something she even wanted. Her life was like a lotus flower: it might be planted in muddy water, but it was still beautiful, fragrant, and pure. Uprooting it would change everything, and she didn't know if she was ready for that.

## Chapter 3:
# The Wisdom of Six

### Sandi

Sedona was attending St. John Bosco Catholic Interparish School (SJB for short), just a couple of miles away from our home, where she was in first grade. The school had a great deal of Southwestern flair: the main building was a large white mission style, and the entrance to the school announced its name in wrought iron letters. The chapel was next to the main gate, and a large cross towered above the statue of St. John Bosco, patron saint of the school. It was a beautiful place for Sedona to go to elementary school, and she was thriving there.

Sedona's first school had been Desert Garden Montessori. We had put her in preschool and kindergarten there because the school had a good reputation, and we wanted her to have the best education we could provide. The philosophy of Montessori is that children will learn when they are ready, and that they need to be self-motivated, which the educators believe children are capable of if they're in a supportive, encouraging environment. While I'm sure this is true for many children, after a couple of years it became clear to Paul and me that it wasn't the right approach for Sedona. She had always been extremely bright, and she wasn't spoiled by any means, but the permissive atmosphere of Desert Garden wasn't having the best effect on her personality.

This was brought home to me one Saturday morning when she was five.

Our weekend ritual began with housework, and for the kids, that meant cleaning their rooms. They were required to pick up their toys, make their beds, and dust their furniture. This was mandatory before they were allowed to play and enjoy their weekend, because Paul and I wanted to instill a sense of responsibility in them. It had never been a problem; usually Sedona cleaned up her room first thing on Saturday morning, so she could get it out of the way. However, this particular Saturday I went into her room to ask her to begin cleaning, and she had an unexpected answer for me.

"Mom, I don't feel like cleaning my room. I feel like watching *SpongeBob*."

I stared at her, dumbfounded.

She said, "When I'm at school I do what I want to do. If I don't feel like reading, I can do something else. Well, now I don't feel like cleaning my room, I feel like watching TV."

That was the day I decided Sedona would attend Catholic school for first grade.

The new environment helped her blossom into an independent, confident, and compassionate child. She loved her brother, her parents, and her animals. Sedona spent many hours mothering her cat and dog and basking in their furry affections. She was introverted by nature, with an ingrained determination that suggested she would accomplish anything she set her mind to. PJ adored her, and so did Paul and I.

—

A day after our initial discussion of Fu Shuang, Paul and I decided to avoid conversations with Sedona about the possible adoption. After all, our daughter was a smart girl and she believed she held most of the cards, which she'd use to her advantage if given half a chance. So, when I picked her up from school, on the way home we chatted about her math homework, and how she had finally completed the perfect cartwheel during recess. I didn't mention Fu Shuang. When Sedona got home, she began her homework, but she looked like something was bothering her. Her normally calm and sweet little face was like a Mexican primrose that had been in the hot desert sun too long – she seemed flushed and wilting.

I had called Sonja and let her know that we needed more time to decide, and while she understood, she also reminded me there was a deadline and it wasn't far off. If we took too long and, in the end, decided not to adopt Fu Shuang, Sonja would have little or no time find another family. However, pressuring Sedona hadn't worked with her in the past – instead she would dig in and become more obstinate. Delightful and caring as my little girl was, she was also extremely stubborn.

As I sat with her this evening, ready to help her with her homework if she needed it, there was a burden in her young eyes, and I knew I was responsible. This adoption drama was a lot for a six-year-old to carry. Paul and I had saddled her with this load, but I didn't see any way around it. This was a family decision and Sedona was an integral part of our family. Paul and I had made our own choices. Now it was up to her.

Once we had started eating dinner, Sedona began to speak.

"I want to talk about Fu Shuang," she said. "Is she in China at her orphanage now?"

"Yes, I imagine she is," Paul said.

"Is she unhappy? Is she hungry? Does she have parents? Does she have friends?"

"We don't really know a lot about her, Sedona," I said. "I can tell you that she doesn't have a family. She doesn't have brothers or sisters. She doesn't have a mother or a father and she's living in an orphanage, like the one you lived in as a baby. Remember the picture I showed you? She lives in northern China and goes to school, and I'm sure she has friends there."

"What will happen to her if she isn't adopted?"

"We don't know," Paul said. "We've heard that often a child who isn't adopted will work in the orphanage after they grow up, but we don't know for sure."

"If she wants to come, we should get her," Sedona said, defiantly lifting her chin as if daring us to argue. "If we don't get her, no one will. After all, I'll still be PJ's older sister, but I'll have an older sister, too. I can handle it. I'm sure I can teach her a thing or two about being an older sister because she doesn't know how to be a sister, but I do. She doesn't know how to be part of a family, but I do. I can teach her how to be part of the Wilson family. Let's go get her."

Because Sedona had declared the decision as worthy, PJ was happy. He was jumping up and down and screaming, "Hurrah!" He looked over at his beautiful sister and smiled. She smiled back.

Paul and I were stunned, speechless. Our wise-beyond-her-years daughter had just let us know that she fully understood, at age six, that if we didn't get this child, Fu Shuang's life wouldn't be complete. She'd let us know that *our* lives wouldn't be complete, and that we needed to move forward with this adoption, fearlessly. We needed to be driven by love.

Thinking how lucky I was to have such remarkable kids, I vowed to call Sonja the next day.

# Chapter 4: Preparing for the Winds of Change

## Sandi

But that night, Paul and I talked about our conversation with Sedona. The focus of our discussion was her statement, "If she wants to come, we should get her."

*Did* Fu Shuang want to come? We had no idea.

It hadn't even occurred to me to wonder, but now I did. This girl was eleven years old and she had her own feelings, ideas, hopes, and dreams. She'd been at the orphanage so long, maybe it had become a kind of home to her. Maybe she wanted to stay where she was. Or maybe she didn't want to be adopted by an American family. Was coming to the United States something she even wanted? We needed to find out.

The transition would be difficult enough with the language barrier and cultural differences; if Fu Shuang wasn't prepared to come, it would be downright impossible.

Fu Shuang would have nothing familiar in this new life. This was not like adopting a baby, since infants and toddlers are able to readily adjust to the change. But even babies had meltdowns and transitional issues, and sometimes had dramatic attachment disorders. The issues would be far greater for an older child dealing with hormones and other trials that come with puberty. Without an active desire to come to America, we didn't know if Fu Shuang could overcome the challenges involved, or if our family would survive this massive change.

The next day I told Sonja the whole story, including all our worries and concerns. We wanted to adopt Fu Shuang, but we felt she had the right to be part of the decision-making process, and we wanted her to *want* to be adopted. We wanted her to be excited and happy about the opportunity to come to America and have a family of her own. If she wasn't, we wouldn't force her. We weren't going to adopt her against her will.

Sonja was silent for a moment, then said, "Okay. I haven't tried this before and I'm not sure if the agency will be able to pull it off, but we can give it a shot. Normally, the children aren't aware that they're going to be adopted until right before it happens. This is to protect the children in case the adoption falls through – we don't want them to get their hopes up for no reason. But this is kind of the opposite situation, so what you want does make sense to me. This is definitely outside of protocol, though, so there's no telling if the orphanage will go along with it. Let me see what I can do."

I was a bundle of nerves – again – but fortunately, I didn't have to wait long to hear from Sonja. When she called back the next day, she immediately let me know she had succeeded. Professor Wu, a Chinese facilitator for Hand-in-Hand, would reach out to the orphanage and talk with the orphanage director. It might take a couple of weeks or longer to work out the details. We were asked to begin the adoption paperwork, with the understanding that if Fu Shuang didn't fully agree to the adoption, it wouldn't proceed.

I was hugely relieved. With this approach, I would feel okay whether the adoption went through or not. Fu Shuang would have the opportunity to decide her own future, and God would help us handle whatever she decided. If she chose to come it would be fated, and if she chose not to, I had to believe China was her destiny, and that the Universe would take care of her.

Paul and I began to pull together our dossier, which consisted of government paperwork, agency forms, home and family pictures, and the completion of our home study. Adoptions are very paper intensive and invasive for the adopting family, as you must prove you'll be able to provide a safe, secure, and positive environment for the child – even if you've been through the process before. Another home study had to be scheduled, which meant our house needed to be prepared and our financial commitment secured, as international adoptions can be very costly. Even though the cost was reduced because Fu Shuang was a special needs adoption, it would put a significant strain on our budget. Coming up with the funding would be tricky, and would require another pull on our second mortgage, as well as maxing out our credit cards for the trip to China.

Our house was another challenge. As Andree had reminded me, we had three bedrooms and needed four, unless the girls shared one. We hated to make the girls share and hadn't brought that up to Sedona yet, since we had a feeling how the idea would go over. We talked about selling the house and buying a bigger one, but financially that wasn't feasible. Originally, our home could've been built with four bedrooms, but we chose the three-bedroom model, thinking we wouldn't have more than one child. Instead of the extra bedroom, we had our house built with a large master suite.

Paul, a "do-it-yourself" kind of guy, decided he could divide our master bedroom into two separate rooms, and create an additional bedroom for Fu Shuang. It was a bittersweet solution because I loved this master bedroom. It had a sitting room with a vaulted ceiling that we used as our office and workout space. A beautiful fireplace in the middle of the room separated the office/workout and sleeping areas, and I had the entire walk-in closet to myself, as Paul used the closet in the adjacent room that we utilized as an office. All of these luxuries would have to go.

From then on, Paul was so busy with the construction project that we barely had time for family activities. Every waking hour when he wasn't at work, he was knocking down walls and making a complete mess. Our bedroom had become a building zone and we slept in dirt and dust. I boxed up our office paperwork and tried to fit all of Paul's clothes and accessories into "my" closet. We wanted to complete the room before the home study, so the pressure was on, and anyone who's ever done home renovation knows how stressful it is. The day Paul tore out the fireplace, I remember thinking I'd never seen such a mess in an occupied home, and I didn't think I could endure it much longer. I began to wonder if the state of our bedroom was indicative of the life challenges we'd face if Fu Shuang joined our family.

Paul was exhausted mentally and physically, with an emphasis on "physically." He was tired, grumpy, and stressed out, and I didn't blame him. When he got home at night, he'd head right to the bedroom and begin his second job. We discussed the construction decision, including the money we were spending to get the room ready. Paul was still very upbeat about bringing Fu Shuang into our lives, but his fatigue was immense, and we were both stretched to our limits – which of course the kids noticed.

Sedona and PJ were irritable because we weren't spending enough time together as a family. I filled out paperwork for the adoption, helped Paul with the master bedroom, and worked on a second home mortgage to fund the adoption. I worried deeply about the monetary commitment, which made everything more difficult. Sedona and PJ were still 100 percent in favor of bringing Fu Shuang into the family and they didn't appear to connect our family issues with her potential arrival, which was a blessing. They just thought Mom and Dad were stressed out.

The new bedroom Paul was creating would become PJ's room, since the door was to open into the master, and he was the youngest. He was excited to be getting a new "big boy" bedroom and planned to leave his baby toys behind. His new room would be bigger and brighter than the room he was vacating, with vaulted ceilings and a large window that looked out onto the backyard and the bright, ocean-blue pool. But at the age of three he still liked having his bedroom attached to Mom and Dad's, for which I was grateful, though I wondered how pleased he'd be when he became a teenager. Still, that was a worry for another day.

It had been a month and we'd still had no answer from China, but we proceeded as though Fu Shuang was coming. It would have felt like tempting fate to change our direction. So we continued our preparations and waited, not so patiently, and told ourselves that it was futile to worry. We tried to live in the moment and enjoy our family, even though we were stressed and covered in drywall dust. If she came, we'd welcome her with all the love in our hearts. If she didn't – well, we'd cross that bridge if we had to.

# Chapter 5: Fu Shuang's Pronouncement

## Fu Shuang

It was springtime and Fu Shuang was at the dreaded boarding school with the other school-age children from the orphanage, as well as other children from around northern China. The Zhaoyang Orphan School in Liaoning Province was a large institution that provided educational services to students from elementary through college level. An estimated thirty-three million children attended boarding schools annually in China at that time. The school was situated in a large, bustling city, but the children weren't allowed to venture out. Fu Shuang felt like a prisoner, just getting through the days, waiting to return to Benxi. She kept her spirits up with daydreams of the green and flourishing countryside back at her home.

This day in early 2004 was like any other day, filled with too much study and not enough comfort. But she had made peace with the status quo, and in its own way, the regular routine, the sameness of her existence, sustained her.

That was about to change.

Fu Lu came running into Fu Shuang's room, saying Mrs. Zhang and Mrs. Wu from their orphanage were downstairs and had come specifically to see Fu Shuang. Fu Lu was a practical joker, so Fu Shuang assumed he was teasing. She wasn't in the mood for his antics, so she tried to ignore him, but he kept chattering about the strangeness of their visit. "What are they doing here? And what do they want with you?"

Eventually, a school administrator called for Fu Shuang to come down and meet her visitors. She was flabbergasted, and even more confused by what they said to her.

"We have some things to talk about," Mrs. Zhang said, "and we'd like to take you out to dinner. We'll be spending the night in a hotel afterward, so go and get some clothes for tomorrow."

"Why are we going?" Fu Shuang asked.

"We'll talk about it later. Go get your things."

This made her very nervous. She'd only ever been out to dinner once and had never spent the night in a hotel. She began to feel that there must be something terribly wrong, though she couldn't begin to guess what it was. She felt she was carrying a fireball in her tummy, but she gathered some clothes, put on a brave face, and followed the caretakers out of the school and into the waiting car.

The restaurant had fabulous food and because Fu Shuang was starving at the boarding school, her concerns took a back seat while she ate.

When her belly was finally full, she said, "I think I ate too much." The very idea amazed her, because it had never happened before. But she was always thoughtful and polite, so despite her shock she said, "Thank you so much for bringing me here. The food was delicious."

"Fu Shuang, we brought you here to ask you a very important question," Mrs. Wu said. "An American couple wants to adopt you, but they want to be sure it's something you desire, because you're old enough to decide. Do you want to be adopted and move to the United States?"

"No!" Fu Shuang said, in a visceral reaction that came to her without thought. Adoption was something the orphanage had rarely discussed with her before, so she'd never considered it a possibility, and her immediate response was that she didn't want to leave Benxi. The orphanage was her home.

The two caregivers spent the rest of the evening at the restaurant trying to convince Fu Shuang that this would be a good move. "You'll have a family, a mom and dad. You'll have a chance for a college education and a better life. In America there are more opportunities for success. Please think about it overnight and we'll discuss it again in the morning," said Mrs. Zhang.

When they retired to the hotel for the night, Fu Shuang couldn't even enjoy the new experience because her mind was spinning. She had so many questions. "If I do this, will I like my mom and dad? Will I have siblings? What will America be like? Will I have nice things? What about my new school, will it be better than the boarding school? What if it's worse? Will I make new friends? Will I be able to learn English? Will I be happier there?"

She had no answers when she finally found sleep. Her night was restless, and she dreamed of parents, siblings, and a home filled with pretty things. In her dream the house was clean and bright and packed with photographs of a smiling family with children – she even saw herself in the pictures. The house felt warm, harmonious, and full of love, and Fu Shuang was filled with happiness.

She woke up with a feeling, an actual knowing, that this was something she needed to do. She couldn't explain how she knew; she just did. Delight filled her spirit. Fu Shuang would be brave and trust that this was her path. She would go to America and have a real family of her own.

At breakfast, Fu Shuang made the declaration that she did want to be adopted. She had been up most of the night wrestling with the question, and even though her eyes were blurry, her heart was certain. Fu Shuang could see her new life in vivid color, filled with rich experiences and deep happiness.

"What changed your mind?" Mrs. Wu said tentatively, almost afraid she'd make Fu Shuang reconsider just by asking.

"I decided I am brave, and I have faith this wouldn't be happening unless it was something I was destined for," Fu Shuang said firmly.

"I'm so proud of you," Mrs. Zhang said, beaming now. "I think you're making the right decision. We'll make sure the American family knows. Remember this day, Fu Shuang. It's the day you stepped into a mystery and created a new life."

# Chapter 6: This Is It

## Sandi

At the end of a busy day filled with out-of-the-office meetings, I found that Sonya had called while I was out. I knew that it was our long-awaited answer from Fu Shuang, so I took a deep breath and began to dial, thinking, *Remember, either way is the right way.* I needed to trust God and the path that opened for our family. Fu Shuang would be on the right path for her life and so would we. If she wasn't coming, then life would return to normal, except half of my once-spacious master bedroom would be sacrificed for a new guest room. If she was coming, then we were in for more preparation, stress, anxiety, and joy – glorious joy.

The moment I heard her pick up at the other end, I jumped in. "Did you hear from Professor Wu?"

"Yes."

I waited for more, but there was none. "Well, was he able to speak with Fu Shuang?"

"Yes."

Sonja's one-word responses made me worry. Fu Shuang didn't want to be adopted. If Sonja had good news, she would have been talking excitedly, wouldn't she? My heart sank. *I guess it's a good thing we asked. I'd hate to bring a kid into our family who didn't want to be with us.* I knew Sedona and PJ would be disappointed, and Paul and I had really been looking forward to meeting the bright-eyed girl who looked back at us from the still photos. But if it wasn't to be, it wasn't to be.

"What happened?" I said, wanting to know the worst.

"Professor Wu spoke with Fu Shuang yesterday. She was at her boarding school with several caretakers from her orphanage. She appeared to be a bit confused when he spoke with her and uncertain about why the American family was asking her opinion. However, in the end she told him yes, she wants to join your family," Sonja said.

Relief flooded my entire being, and I almost didn't hear the rest of what Sonja had to say.

"She's a very direct girl, outgoing and honest. She told him that at first she was uncertain, but after carefully considering the impact it would have on her life, she had decided to be adopted. She wants to come, she wants a family, and she wants to be an American."

"Oh my gosh! Thank you, Sonja! Thank you so much for working with us on this," I said in a rush. I had been holding my breath for so long that I felt light-headed, ready to pass out from lack of oxygen. "I've been so nervous – we've all been nervous – and we've tried not to worry but –" Paul, Sedona, PJ, and I would finally be able to take a deep, cleansing breath and allow ourselves to get properly excited. "I can't wait to tell Paul and the kids! The Wilsons will be celebrating tonight," I said, laughing with delight.

Sonja and I congratulated each other, exchanged some squeals of joy, and said goodbye. I knew that I had a lot more paperwork, financial preparation, and home adjustments to make, but I was relieved and very, very grateful.

I hung up the phone and immediately dialed Paul. He was elated and suggested we all go out to dinner that night to celebrate our good fortune. We would toast Fu Shuang – our double luck girl and the soon-to-be newest member of the Wilson clan.

—

We went to Golden City, a little Chinese restaurant in a strip mall by our house. It was a small, locally owned place Sedona loved. The interior was set in the traditional red of China, with Chinese sayings throughout the room and a big poster celebrating the "Year of the Monkey." The golden Chinese Lucky Cat waved to us as we entered the establishment, and I grinned at it. This lucky cat has its origin in Japan, not China, but is often seen in Chinese restaurants and is called Maneki Neko. The waving arm on the cat is believed to be gesturing for good luck. Such a great symbol for celebrating "Luck times Two" joining our family.

I wanted to recognize Sedona for her wisdom and her honesty, since she was the one who cast the deciding vote and was greatly responsible for this adoption materializing. She wore a bright yellow dress with purple leggings, her deep black hair cropped to her shoulders, bangs hanging over her dark, sparkling eyes. She glowed with pleasure as we made a fuss over her for her role in the proceedings.

Paul and I explained our plans to go to China to bring their new sister home. They were both excited about meeting Fu Shuang, and even PJ seemed to understand the big step that this was, and how much it would change our family.

"Are we going to go to China with you?" PJ asked, his bright face beaming with anticipation.

"I'm afraid not, sweetie," I said.

"Why not?" A pout formed on his usually sweet face.

"The flight takes over twenty hours and it's too expensive to bring everyone. We'll only be gone for a couple of weeks, and we'll bring your new sister home with us," Paul said. "You're going to stay with Grandma and Andree, and they're going to have all kinds of fun things for you to do. We'll call you from China once we get there and meet Fu Shuang."

PJ started to cry. "I don't want to stay home. I want to go with you."

This was the beginning of a difficult road with PJ. He hadn't been away from us since we'd brought him home from Guatemala, so this was understandably a huge deal for him. He was scared and it made him peevish. As we continued to make preparations in the coming weeks, he required frequent reassurance.

But that night, Sedona looked crossly at him with all the superiority of a big sister. "PJ, we don't want to go to China. It's a long, boring trip. Let's stay home with Grandma. It'll be better. I promise."

PJ's trust in Sedona was absolute, but sniffled, and large teardrops ran down his sweet, chubby cheeks. Finally, as she continued to radiate assurance, he tentatively said, "Okay. We'll have fun without Mom and Dad, right?"

"That's *right*," she said.

I had never been more grateful for her sisterly authority.

## Chapter 7: The Waiting Game

### Fu Shuang

Even after the decision was made, the adoption process was slow, and months went by while Fu Shuang waited for her new adventure. She constantly thought about leaving China. She speculated about her new life and the changes that were coming her way. She imagined a big house with a television, a large family with grandparents and aunts and uncles, new friends, a wonderful school, and lots and lots of happiness. She and her school friends talked about life in America, wondering how different it would be. Did they play any of the same games? What kind of food did they eat? How did they dress? The questions were never-ending, and since she didn't have any of the answers, sometimes her fears took over.

*Maybe I won't like it. Maybe they won't like me.* But whenever her thoughts turned negative, she considered what a miracle it was that she was being adopted at her age.

*This must mean I'm meant to be with this family*, she'd tell herself, and her fears would subside.

She knew the culture of the United States was very different from China. Movie stars, music legends, and television celebrities lived in this rich land. Fu Shuang wondered if she might be close to the action, living in Hollywood or New York, the most famous American cities. She thought all Americans had money and imagined that would apply to her own life: she'd have nice clothes and toys she didn't have to share, her stomach would no longer be empty, and her fortunes would be reversed. She had heard people call America "The Land of Opportunity," and since she was becoming an American citizen, her future would be bright. *She* would be one of the world's fortunate people.

One chilly autumn evening while she waited for her adoption to be finalized, Fu Shuang was outside the boarding school with friends during their dinner break. The sun hadn't set, but it hung low in the sky, as it prepared to disappear below the horizon. The children wandered around, getting in a little activity before they had to go back inside. Fu Shuang lost her balance on the concrete, which was icy in the cold. She slipped and fell flat on her back, landing hard on her tailbone. The pain was so severe her friends had to help her up. She tried to walk it off but the pain persisted, so the other children helped her to the nurse's office.

When they arrived, the nurse appeared occupied, so the children left Fu Shuang and went on their way. The nurse gestured for Fu Shuang to sit down. She sat – gingerly – and began to tell the nurse what had happened. The nurse listened intently, but without warning the nurse's boyfriend barged into the room. He was a large man with broad shoulders and an angry scowl. He towered over Fu Shuang and glared at the nurse, who tried to get him to leave the exam area and wait for her in the next room. But he wasn't having any of it. He began screaming obscenities and gesticulating wildly.

The nurse was clearly embarrassed, concerned that the school administrators would hear the commotion and discover her irate boyfriend in the examination room.

Since she clearly couldn't control him, she turned to Fu Shuang. "Can't you see I'm busy? You don't look hurt to me. Go away and don't come back."

Fu Shuang left the room in excruciating pain and hobbled back to her room, stopping to rest several times along the way. Her back wasn't just sore. A pervasive stinging, burning sensation radiated outward from her spine and filled her entire body.

She didn't know what she'd injured, but she knew she'd damaged something, because although the agony died down after a few days, she went through the next several months with a constant pain in her tailbone. She was too afraid to go back to the nurse, so she suffered in silence. It was one more reason she wouldn't miss this horrible place.

Finally, several months after Fu Shuang's decision to be adopted, her orphanage caretakers showed up on the steps of the boarding school. They had never visited her school before, as far as she knew, and now they'd come twice in three months – both times to see her. This time, Fu Shuang knew they had come to take her back to the orphanage, where she would wait until it was time to meet her new parents.

When she saw Mrs. Zhang and Mrs. Wu, her spirits rose. They had always been kind to her, and they were here to help her start preparing for her new life. They spoke excitedly about her adoption for a few minutes, then Mrs. Zhang said, "Pack up your things and say your goodbyes to your teachers and friends. You won't be back here again."

Fu Shuang's excitement turned abruptly to melancholy as the finality of her decision sank in. *I'll never see my friends again. I'll be living with strangers in a strange country. I'm not an American, I'm Chinese. I belong in China. What have I done?* Her sadness was as profound as it was sudden, and she began to cry.

Mrs. Zhang and Mrs. Wu both looked at her with concern, then at each other. Mrs. Wu pulled out a package. "This is from your new family," she said, handing it to Fu Shuang. "I think you should open it."

Fu Shuang sat down and examined the package. It was a large box wrapped in brown paper, covered with official-looking forms and stamps. She looked more closely at the stamps in the upper right-hand corner and noticed "USA 37." The stamps had Chinese writing and a rainbow-colored monkey that seemed to stare straight at her. The stamps said "Happy New Year" in Chinese and what she assumed was English. She felt relieved to know that Americans also celebrated her favorite holiday, and her tears stopped. She began to carefully open the box.

As she peeled away the paper, she thought about the monkey on the stamp. According to the Chinese zodiac, this was the Year of the Monkey. She had been born a Monkey in 1992, which meant 2004 was the first Year of the Monkey since her birth, and what a year it was turning out to be. Monkeys were considered clever, lively, intelligent, enthusiastic, and mischievous. Fu Shuang thought the sign of the monkey fit her personality. She also thought it was significant that she was to begin a new life during her astrological year.

When she opened the package sent by the Americans, the first thing she saw was a small, sleek, silver camera. She looked for the film that should go with the camera; there was none to be found. "How can I take pictures without film?" she asked. Mrs. Wu explained that the camera was digital: no film needed. Fu Shuang was delighted. Now she could take pictures of her home, her friends, and her beloved China before she left, so she would never forget. "I'm going to take pictures of everything," she told Mrs. Zhang and Mrs. Wu.

Next, she unwrapped a simple white T-shirt, just her size. It had a rectangular print on it with white stars on a blue background in the left corner and red and white stripes below and to the right of the stars. She realized it represented the flag of the United States and smiled to think she'd be wearing an American T-shirt.

After carefully folding the shirt, she took a small blue box out of the package. It looked like there was something very special inside. Fu Shuang opened the hinged top and saw a small analog watch on a purple band with pink flowers. She loved it immediately. The time on the watch was wrong, but she put it on anyway. Never in her life had she owned any jewelry and she gazed at her wrist in admiration, grinning as she turned it this way and that.

*I haven't even met them yet, and they've already given me more than I have ever owned.*

Finally, she removed a book from the box and moved to the sofa to be alone while she perused the pages. It was a scrapbook of sorts, with a beautiful and colorful jacket that had flowers and butterflies laid out like a quilt tapestry. When she opened it, she was ecstatic. It was filled with pictures of her life-to-be. The first picture was a two-story pink home she thought looked gigantic. Would that really be *her* house? There were loads of pictures of her new mom and dad, her new brother and sister, her new grandma and grandpa, and other family and friends who would most likely play roles in her life. She knew she'd still miss China and all her friends at the orphanage, but now the unknowns of her future seemed a little less scary. She would have a family who wanted her, and a home of her own. She wouldn't have to stay at a boarding school for ten months a year. She would have plenty to eat and clothes that belonged only to her.

She looked at Mrs. Zhang and Mrs. Wu, who watched her intently. She smiled her crooked smile. Relieved, they smiled back.

## Chapter 8:
# So Long, Boarding School

### Fu Shuang

Fu Shuang had known she'd have to say goodbye to people she loved, but now the time had come and the pain was unexpectedly sharp. Her heart beat a little too fast, her chest tightened, and she began to take small shallow breaths. She wasn't ready for this, but she was determined to be courageous.

The day was a whirlwind of activities. She said farewell to friends and teachers, and as she'd promised, took pictures of everything and everyone. She loved China, and never wanted to forget the beauty and good times. She didn't have much to pack since her clothes all belonged to the orphanage, but she did have the watch and T-shirt her new parents had given her. She was cheerful and determined. Her friends congratulated her on her good fortune, and her teachers told her to keep up her studies.

On Fu Shuang's last night, she was given the choice of staying with her friends in the dormitory or going to a hotel with her caretakers. For Fu Shuang it was an easy choice – she'd spend her last hours at the boarding school with her friends. The school was very strict about talking at night, but the children whispered and giggled in their smallest voices and didn't sleep at all. The night was filled with hope and joy, devoid of sadness. Fu Shuang had asked everyone to leave her with only happy memories, and so they did.

The next day, dressed in green flowered capri pants, her USA flag shirt, and sandals with socks, Fu Shuang began her journey. Her short, dark hair was in pigtails and her face beamed. Though she was worried and sad inside, she did her best to appear her usual confident, happy, and playful self.

The morning of her departure, she gave her biggest smile and hug to Fu Lu. Fu Shuang considered him not just a lifelong friend but also a brother, and losing his companionship was painful in the extreme. His name meant "double happiness" and that was what she wished for him.

As she gave him a final squeeze, she whispered, "You're going to be adopted too. Your family will be here soon. Always remember me and our years together. Remember me whenever you think of China."

"I will always recall our time together, Fu Shuang. You're my best friend and my sister. Take care and have a good life," he said with tears in his eyes.

With those words, she got into the sedan that would whisk her back to the orphanage, where she would say goodbyes all over again to the younger children and her caregivers.

When she got into the car, she waved goodbye and smiled to her friends. However, as they lurched onto the road where they couldn't see, the waterworks opened up. She let the tears come for over an hour before she decided enough was enough. She took a deep breath and straightened up in the seat. Her composure returned, and her affability resumed as they drove on. *I have nothing to fear. I will remember my old friends and make new ones. And I will love my new life.* Her determination and resilience took control and brought her back to the optimism that was her fundamental character.

The trip back to Benxi was long, but the drive was pleasant. Fu Shuang was given the opportunity to stop and see several sights along the way. She saw large government buildings and historical monuments, charming countryside homes and miles of green grass, rice fields, and wildflowers. They visited large cities and rural villages on this day-long adventure. Every site seemed to proclaim the glory of China. Fu Shuang took it all in, trying to soak up as much of her homeland as she could before leaving it for what could be forever.

When it was close to lunchtime, Mrs. Zhang said, "Let's stop at McDonald's and get Fu Shuang a hamburger and fries."

"What a wonderful idea," Mrs. Wu said. "Fu Shuang, how would you like to try out American food for lunch?"

"I'd love it!" Fu Shuang said with great excitement. Then she thought for a moment. "What kind of food do the Americans eat anyway?"

"You'll see," they said in unison, grinning.

They could see the golden arches from many miles down the road. When they pulled into the parking lot, Fu Shuang thought the building was strange and that the smells coming from the restaurant were not appetizing. She had little experience with restaurants in general and had never been to a fast-food chain. McDonald's was packed with customers on this sunny day, most of whom appeared to be enjoying the food in front of them as they chatted with their companions. There were chicken nuggets, hamburgers, chicken sandwiches, sodas, and French fries. It all looked so strange to Fu Shuang. A greasy smell hung in the air, which to her was heavy and unpleasant.

Mrs. Wu ordered for Fu Shuang without asking her opinion. Fu Shuang would try a hamburger and French fries, the ultimate American food.

When the order arrived, Fu Shuang stared at it. It didn't look or smell appealing and she was suddenly not very hungry. She looked dubiously at the items on her tray.

"You'll like it," Mrs. Wu said. "It's delicious."

Fu Shuang put a French fry into her month and slowly chewed. *Not bad.* Then she took a bite of the hamburger, and almost immediately spit it out onto the wrapper. "This is horrible," she said loudly. She frowned and put the hamburger down in a rare exhibition of preteen attitude. "Do I have to eat it?"

"You need to eat as much as you can. This is your lunch," Mrs. Wu said. "Do you like the French fries? Do you like your Coca-Cola? Eat and drink them, at least."

As she sipped at her soda and nibbled at her fries, Fu Shuang felt this was not a promising start. She thought that after her adoption she'd never be hungry again, but it might be just like her boarding school, where the only food she was offered, she couldn't stand to eat. But she wasn't going to let it ruin her day or her hope for the future. *I'm sure I can find something good to eat in America – at least I know I like French fries and Coke.* If there was one thing Fu Shuang knew how to do, it was go hungry.

## Chapter 9:
# What's in a Name?

### Sandi

Preparations for Fu Shuang's arrival continued. This was a hectic time for the family, and while Paul had the most challenging responsibility – finishing the fourth bedroom – pretty much everything else fell to me. I oversaw decorating Fu Shuang's room, getting her new clothes, buying gifts for the orphanage and their staff, making travel arrangements, and finalizing the paperwork. But one critical element Paul and I needed to address together: picking an American name for Fu Shuang.

With both Sedona and PJ we had chosen new first names and used their birth names as their middle names. When we got Sedona her first name was *Lican* (pronounced LEE-

CON), which means "beautiful and splendid." Since my middle name is Lee, in a way Sedona and I shared a name, which created a special bond between us. Her adopted and permanent name is Sedona Lican Wilson.

PJ's birth name was José, which means "may God increase." In English José translates as Joseph, which was my father's name, creating another kind of family bond. His adopted and permanent name is Parker José Wilson, but we began calling him "PJ" early on, and it stuck.

Picking a name for Sedona seemed impossible at first. During the international adoption process, the parents must specify a name for the adoptive child before ever meeting them, so all we had to go on were photographs. In pictures Sedona was as beautiful and splendid as her Chinese name, and we wanted her American name to reflect that. It was a tall order, and Paul and I were really having a hard time with it. Then, right before we were to turn in the paperwork, we took a weekend trip to Sedona, Arizona.

Paul and I are both natives of Arizona and we love to take trips to various cities and towns around the state; Sedona is one of our favorites. It's a small town about a hundred miles north of Phoenix and is a spiritual focal point, surrounded by the stunning natural beauty of the area. This trip was going to be our last without our new daughter and we wanted to enjoy private time together in a place we loved.

When you drive into Sedona, you are met by an extraordinary topography. It almost looks like you're driving into the heart of the Grand Canyon, but upside down – the red rock formations are mountains rather than valleys. It's both magical and majestic. Whenever we're in Sedona, we're at peace.

During the high climb from the desert floor to the Verde Valley where Sedona is located, Paul and I talked about new names for Lican. We considered the name Rio from the Duran Duran song, because it was pretty, and the lyrics seemed to fit how we felt about our new daughter. But much as we liked the song, it referenced the Rio Grande, which doesn't run through Arizona, and we wanted a name that was reflective of *our* Southwest and the state that would be her new home. So, we kept trying ideas, but none of the more traditional names we came up with resonated with us.

Then, as we drove into the city of Sedona it dawned on us: why not name her after one of our favorite places in the whole world? Sedona itself is beautiful and splendid. Red rock spires and buttes are set against endless, deep blue skies. Cacti and small brush grow among piñon pines, and the smell of all this high-desert greenery is fresh and crisp. The land is filled with adventure, but still offers peace and tranquility. Yes, Sedona would be her name.

And so, it became our tradition to use Arizona names for our children. When it came time to name José, we simply opened the map of Arizona and found the name we wanted. Parker, Arizona, is a small town on the Colorado River, close to Lake Havasu City, where we had a second home at the time. In Parker, the purple mountains reach to the cloudless sky, towering above the stark desert terrain. The blue of the river cuts through the bleached desert sand, sparkling in the sun. It's hard to describe the feeling you get looking at water in the desert. It's not just beautiful or picturesque; it's inspirational, hopeful. It seemed the perfect name for our new son, who had already survived so much.

Now it was time to find a name for Fu Shuang.

We brought out the map again. In southern Arizona there's town called Sierra Vista, which means "mountain range view" – the range in this case being the Huachuca Mountains. An adoptive family we knew had named their daughter Sierra about the time we adopted Sedona, and we had always loved the name. We began talking about the name as a possibility, and it suddenly came together: the Huachuca range has a pronounced double mountain peak, which seemed to us to represent the "luck times two" of Fu Shuang's name. Sierra is also an Irish name, the feminine of Ciaran, meaning "dark." This may be an unorthodox comparison, but it did fit with Fu Shuang's jet-black hair and dark piercing eyes. Our soon-to-be daughter's name would be Sierra Fu Shuang Wilson.

Now all that was left was to go to China and bring her home.

While our hearts were overflowing with love for our new daughter, there was also a large amount of fear. Fu Shuang was coming to us with a developed personality and was much older than any child we had parented. As much as I wanted her to become a member of our little tribe, I knew her presence would alter the energy and the dynamics of the whole family, but I didn't know *how*, or how much. I felt that she would improve all our lives as much as I hoped we'd improve hers, but in truth there was no telling what would happen once she became a Wilson. It was impossible to predict how this might reshape her, our family, and our future. I prayed that Paul and I would be able to handle the transformation that was upon us, and that Sierra would fit into our family like a missing puzzle piece.

# Chapter 10: China Mist

## Fu Shuang

It was the beginning of Autumn 2004 and Fu Shuang had been waiting in Benxi for her parents to pick her up for several months. The older children were away at boarding school, so Fu Shuang spent her time caring for the younger kids and assisting the caregivers. She was responsible for feeding the babies, changing diapers, and helping with meal preparation and kitchen clean-up. It was a lot of responsibility for a twelve-year-old and she missed her friends, but she enjoyed playing with the toddlers and she was usually too busy to feel sad. With the rest of the older kids gone, Fu Shuang became an extension of the staff.

The mornings started off at 5:00 a.m. when Fu Shuang went to the kitchen to help prepare breakfast. The syrupy smell of sugar filled the room each morning as the kids ate sticky rice and a sweet bun with water for their first meal. After breakfast, Fu Shuang went to the nursery when babies were waking up, hungry and fussy. Fu Shuang hurried about, changing diapers, getting the infants cleaned up and dressed, and giving them their bottles. It was a lot of work, but she liked being useful and she loved to look into the babies' curious eyes. They seemed to be trying to figure out the world, just as she was.

After the nursery duties, she was allowed a break to watch TV in the great room until lunchtime, when she again helped in the kitchen. Her favorite show was called *Emperor Warrior*, an action show for older kids, but she also watched *Teletubbies* and Disney cartoons with the younger children.

As lunchtime approached, the smell of the food permeated the building, and Fu Shuang tried to guess what was going to be served even as she hurried to the kitchen to help the kitchen staff. Meals included fish, dumplings, chicken feet or necks, egg drop soup, rice balls, sticky rice, or sauerkraut. There was never a lot of food, but with so many of the other children away, the chef gave her a larger portion and she was often able to eat her fill.

The younger children napped in the afternoon, so Fu Shuang could go to the playground, the store, or just go outside and walk around. The park across the street from the orphanage was beautiful this time of year, as autumn was taking hold. She thought there must be every color imaginable: forest-green pines, green grass, and dark green ferns were interspersed with leaves turning harvest yellow, burnt orange, red, and even purple. The park's playground had swings, a slide, and a merry-go-round, and it was popular with children from the neighborhood after school. Fu Shuang missed kids her own age, but because these children were strangers, she wasn't allowed to make friends or even talk to them – it was against the Institute's rules. As gregarious and outgoing as she was, she found this a difficult rule to follow, especially since she was lonely. But she tried to content herself with rocking on the swing set and daydreaming about her new life, hoping she'd make lots of friends in America and have the freedom to talk to anyone and everyone. Fu Shuang planned to surround herself with new people and learn American ways. In her mind's eye she could see a whole new girl, surrounded by family and being loved. *I can't wait to begin my new life and expand my knowledge. I am so lucky.*

The waiting was hard on her, and occasionally her mood darkened. She desperately wanted to get on with it. She wasn't often downcast, but there was a small part of her personality that was prone to melancholy, and when this shadow appeared, she tended to clam up and dwell on negative thoughts. *This might be the biggest blunder I've ever made. Maybe I won't like* anything *there. The food, the language, the people will be so foreign I can't even imagine. I love China and I'm sorry to be leaving. I hope I don't hate it there. If I ever even* get *there.*

The weather in Benxi was temperate, but wet. This autumn the high temperatures were in the sixties and there was quite a bit of rain, so everything around her was exceptionally green and lush. The orphanage seemed surrounded with fragrant flowers and stately trees, and as she walked the grounds, she drank in the beauty of her beloved China. With the fall foliage on display, she felt the land itself was saying goodbye. Leaving China was bittersweet.

—

One day Mrs. Zhang took Fu Shuang home with her. She thought it would help Fu Shuang get ready for life outside the walls of the orphanage. Mrs. Zhang oversaw business and marketing at the orphanage, and she had become attached to Fu Shuang. Fu Shuang and Fu Lu were her "go-to" kids whenever she brought potential financial contributors to the orphanage, because they were so charming and entertaining. She knew she was going to miss this clever, funny, cheerful little girl, and she decided having Fu Shuang stay for a couple of days would be good for both of them.

Mrs. Zhang had a husband and a fifteen-year-old daughter. Their house was very small, but immaculate. It had a living room, one bedroom, one bath, and a kitchen. Mrs. Zhang's daughter slept in the living room, and so did Fu Shuang. They cooked food together in the evening, and everyone shared in cleaning up. The family took Fu Shuang shopping and showed her around their neighborhood. They all enjoyed the visit, which Fu Shuang found as helpful as Mrs. Zhang had hoped. When she saw that the way families lived was much like the orphanage, just on a much smaller scale, Fu Shuang began to better understand what her future would look like. She was grateful for the experience and began to get excited about her new life. She would be the oldest child in the family, so she would be looking after her brother and sister, like she did with the young kids at her orphanage. She would have chores, duties, and responsibilities, just like she did here, and her life would still be important – she would have a purpose. Being useful mattered to her, so these thoughts were encouraging.

—

After months of waiting, there was still no news on exactly when her parents would be arriving, and Fu Shuang became convinced they had changed their minds and weren't coming. She knew adoption was never certain. She'd seen it herself when kids who were supposed to be adopted instead remained at the orphanage. She also knew this was her only chance because of her advanced age. But she kept the uncertainty to herself. However, as worried she was on the inside, on the outside she appeared confident, cheery, and ready for the change.

One afternoon Fu Shuang was in the nursery after lunch, putting the infants down for their nap. She was rubbing the back of a baby boy who was fussing when Mrs. Wu rushed into the room.

"Your parents are here, Fu Shuang!"

Fu Shuang was stunned into immobility. She stood motionless and unable to focus.

"You need to shower, put on clean clothes, and get ready. You're going to Shenyang to meet them this afternoon," Mrs. Wu said, ushering her out of the nursery.

Fu Shuang couldn't believe it. After all this time, it was happening *now.*

Still dazed, she ran to the showers, and in her excitement she almost slipped and fell. The water was cold and as it hit her skin she began to shiver. The wait was over, but the journey was just beginning. Her emotions were in such turmoil she began to cry, her tears mixing with the water washing over her. She was cold and shivering but her face felt flushed, so she stood a little longer and let the water cool her. Scared, sad, excited, and still stunned, Fu Shuang got ready to meet her new parents.

She had to say more sorrowful goodbyes, and they still wouldn't be the last. After more hugs and tears with the younger children and farewells to the staff, she braced herself for the trip to the big city and the start of her new life. One of the staff gave her an orange cream frozen treat for the trip. The cool sweetness calmed her, and she began to shake off her sadness and fear. She yearned for a life filled with adventure, happiness, and friendship. She hoped she would be loved by her new family and that she would love them too.

The trip would take an hour, and once she arrived, she would meet her mother and father. With misty eyes, Fu Shuang began the last leg of her journey as an orphan.

# Chapter 11: Meeting Fate

## Sandi

When we arrived at our hotel in Shenyang, China, we'd been traveling for over twenty hours. The city was enormous, strikingly modern, and densely populated. The towering skyscrapers were colorful, and the city was obviously growing; everywhere we looked, green bamboo scaffolding clung to the columns of gigantic buildings in progress. Older constructions with traditional architecture were interspersed with more modern structures, a common sight in many a Chinese metropolis.

Shenyang seemed to go on forever. It's the provincial capital of the Liaoning Province, with 6.3 million residents, and is one of China's most important industrial cities. While

Paul and I had been to several urban areas in China when we adopted Sedona, this city was different. Last time, we'd visited tourist-friendly Hong Kong and Shanghai, and these impressive cities seemed to represent the high-end business and financial centers of the nation, rather than industrial. Shenyang was clearly a working city, without a lot of foreign visitors. It didn't feel as welcoming as the China we remembered from 1998.

I was so exhausted after the hours and hours of travel that all I could really think of was sleep. We were staying at the Crowne Plaza Shenyang, a twenty-year-old building located in the heart of the city. It was a model hotel, built of white concrete with mirrored glass windows, and was adjacent to the government buildings that would facilitate the completion of our adoption. The hotel was filled with amenities, but at the time we didn't care. The only thing we wanted was a comfortable bed. We checked into the hotel and headed straight to our room, where we both immediately fell into slumber, even though it was morning in Shenyang.

It seemed we had only shut our eyes for a minute when the phone rang. Paul groggily answered. "Hello. Okay, thank you. When? Right. Please call us when they arrive."

I kept my head down hoping I could just go back to sleep.

"Sandi, you need to get up. The orphanage officials are on their way to the hotel with Fu Shuang," he said.

I groaned. "You've got to be kidding. I'm too tired to meet her today." Don't get me wrong, I was desperate to meet Fu Shuang and usher her into the bosom of our loving family, but I'm the kind of person who needs sleep to function, and when I don't get it, I'm cranky. Now I was exhausted and hostile, which wasn't what I'd had in mind for the day I'd meet our new daughter. Why did they have to bring her *now?*

But now was when she was coming, whether we were prepared or not, and Paul wasn't going to let me be a grouch. "Get up and stop whining," he said. "She'll be here in about half an hour. Splash your face with water and let's get ready to meet our new daughter."

"Okay, okay," I grumbled. I was like a zombie as I got out of bed and headed for the shower, but the cool water began to wake me up. It started to sink in that Fu Shuang would be with us soon, and all my worries came crashing in. When we'd adopted Sedona and PJ, I'd been both excited and nervous, but this was more like terror. This meeting would be very different from our first two adoption encounters. Sedona and PJ were babies when we'd met them; Fu Shuang was almost a teenager.

When we adopted Sedona, we'd been impatiently waiting at the hotel until they picked us up to take us to the government building where we would meet her. A government official handed her to Paul. She scowled at him, bawling at full volume. He looked at her and immediately handed her over to me. To my surprise, she stopped crying, and although there were still tears rolling down her fat baby cheeks, she quieted and fell asleep within ten minutes. She was so beautiful, so perfect, I couldn't stop looking at her.

Parker's first meeting with us was completely different. PJ's foster family and our adoption facilitator brought him to our hotel and his reaction was the opposite of Sedona's

– he was alert and playful. He gurgled, as babies do, smiled, clapped his hands, and hugged his foster sisters. Paul and I were both able to hold him and he was quite content. His foster family – mother, grandfather, and sisters – wept as they left because they'd grown so fond of him, but PJ was fine. He was fearless and happy.

With Fu Shuang it would be a distinctly new experience. We would have a preteen who wouldn't be able to communicate effectively with us. She might be moody, terrified, or both. We hadn't parented an older child and we didn't know what to expect, and so my panic seemed justified in the moment.

Dread grew as I waited for the phone to ring. When it did, Paul and I both jumped, and after he had a quick exchange through the phone, we headed downstairs to the lobby. My heart beat violently, and my head ached from anxiety and lack of sleep. I felt like I had been thrashed during the night – physically battered and emotionally exhausted. But I was soon to be Fu Shuang's mother and that obligation had already rooted deep inside, so I took a few deep breaths and called up reserves of energy I didn't know I had.

—

It was September 26, 2004, and the Crowne Plaza Hotel bustled with people. Deliverymen brought food to the Lin de Court restaurant during the noon hour. The restaurant served Chinese cuisine as well as Western-influenced food, and we could hear the clinking of plates, silverware, and glasses on the second floor as we walked into the lobby.

We were rushed into a taxi and taken to an office building to meet Fu Shuang. The building was old and very governmental, with dull gray asbestos-filled tiles on the floor, tan metal desks that looked like they came straight out of the 1970s, the smell of sour mildew, and papers piled everywhere.

As we strolled through the front door, we saw two middle-aged Chinese women with a little Chinese girl. Even in my fatigue and worry, I felt a thrill of joy. "That's our daughter," I said to Paul, smiling.

Fu Shuang wore an orange long sleeve shirt trimmed in navy blue with the number "3" printed on the front. *The third child added to our family*, I thought.

Three is significant in numerology and in many religions of the world. It represents harmony, wisdom, and understanding. It represents time as past, present, and future; and beginning, middle, and end. It's the number of the divine. In Christianity, it's the trinity: Father, Son, and Holy Spirit. In Hinduism, it represents the Trimurti, the three Gods of the Hindu triad. In Buddhism, it represents the three jewels: Buddha, Dharma, and Sangha. Looking back on her entrance into my life, I find it fascinating that Fu Shuang wore the number "3" and can't help but surmise it as a sign that she was divinely intended to join our family.

She also sported khaki pants that had "NBA" printed on the front. At first, I thought this stood for the National Basketball Association, but later realized it wasn't an American reference at all and we never found out the meaning. Her white canvas shoes had little elastic straps to hold them onto her feet. Her gleaming black hair had been plaited into tiny braids tied with colorful hair bands, gathered around her lovely oval face and pulled up into two pig tails on each side of her head. She looked adorable, but she wasn't smiling. She seemed composed but watchful.

As I look back at the picture of the three of us on that day in September, I think we were all in shock. We were about to become a family, yet we were strangers. I was petrified that we might be making a mistake, and I think Fu Shuang was too. We wouldn't be able to mold this child – her personality and habits were already largely formed. This relationship would not be built on the gradual uphill road of childhood and the trust the parent/child relationship establishes over time.

Not only that, but we'd have to find our way without a common language, making the whole process that much more difficult. It was going to be like beginning a journey in the middle of the roadway, with traffic coming from each direction, and all the signs in hieroglyphics. But I knew that despite the challenges, we would find our way. Paul and I smiled at Fu Shuang, and she gave us a small, hesitant smile in return, but I could see she was as worried as we were.

We signed a lot of paperwork, printed in Chinese and English. The Chinese text was written in pinyin, the system for writing Chinese with Roman letters. Pinyin includes extra marks to denote tones, and with my blurred, fatigued vision, all of them appeared to be moving. I was so tired that the pinyin words not only looked like little pine trees, houses, smiley faces, tic-tac-toe squares, and other interesting shapes, but they were totally animated and telling me a story I was too dense to understand.

The officials took our picture with Fu Shuang, and this became our first family photo. We paid the caretakers the required $3,000 donation for the orphanage and left with our soon-to-be daughter. There would be more bureaucratic hoops to jump through, but we were on our way. It felt good, but unreal.

Because Fu Shuang could not speak English and we could not speak Chinese, the day was bizarre. The orphanage officials left, and we returned to the hotel room. We gave Fu Shuang the clothes we had brought, along with a personal CD player and a couple of CDs. We introduced her to Pringles potato chips. She loved them and probably ate too many, but we didn't care. We were just happy that she was eating something – she was a skinny little thing. She loved the CD player and sat on her bed for hours, listening to her new albums. Little did we know just how much she cherished music; she'd have earbuds in her ears from then on.

We also noticed there was something wrong with Fu Shuang's back. It was curved at her tailbone, making her posture unnaturally twisted. This was not part of the health information we'd received from China and would need to be diagnosed once she returned to the States. For her sake, we hoped it wasn't painful, but we had no way to ask her.

That night, we ate at the hotel's restaurant, Lin de Court. Fu Shuang clearly wasn't used to eating out, but she ordered from the menu without our help while Paul and I struggled to understand the descriptions well enough to order for ourselves. Having been to China before, we knew most waiters and waitresses were able to speak at least some English, so we asked for assistance. After our orders had been taken, we wished we could have kept the waitress there as a translator; it was strange having Fu Shuang with us and not being able to speak with her. Dinner was tasty, but awkward.

Afterward, back to the room we went. We were exhausted physically and emotionally, but we had made it through the day, and we felt strangely encouraged by Fu Shuang. While we couldn't converse with her, I could feel her positive energy and it felt good to be in her company.

Fu Shuang watched TV as Paul and I spoke about the future and prayed that everything would work out with our new daughter. Finally, it was time to turn off the lights and go to bed. I was drained, more tired than I could ever remember being, but more sanguine about the future than I had been for months. The process had started, and tomorrow we would continue to get to know Sierra Fu Shuang Wilson.

# Chapter 12: What Comes Next?

## Fu Shuang

Fu Shuang's impression of her first day with her new parents was different. The ride from the orphanage to Shenyang was about an hour, and to her it was like a beautiful symphony, her thoughts building from nervous excitement to full-out joy. She still felt some apprehension, but the fact that her adoption was actually happening had released the tension of the last several months. She felt like she had been wearing a straight jacket and the buckles had finally been freed. As the American couple approached her for the first time in that shabby government building, she said to her caretakers, "There are my parents. They're really here and

I'm really going to America." When they smiled at her, she smiled back.

When they were introduced, her new mom kissed her forehead, which Fu Shuang thought was weird. Affection was not something she'd been given in large doses, so this action made her uncomfortable. Her father shook her hand. These people were so foreign to her they might as well have been aliens, and soon she would fly across the globe to live her life with these strange beings from another world.

The day was filled with paperwork, picture-taking, fingerprinting, and other tedious bureaucratic tasks. Fu Shuang couldn't wait to leave and move on with her life. She'd been told she'd be sent to the hotel with her new parents and would spend her first night with them there. Before the group was to leave, Mrs. Wu and Mrs. Zhang told Fu Shuang her new name. She tried to say it out loud, but the combination of sounds was unfamiliar to her mouth, and it wouldn't come out right. But she thought it sounded pretty when the others said it.

The office building was close to the hotel, so the trip in the taxi was quick. The Crowne Plaza was massive, grand, and filled with new sights and sounds. There were businessmen and women, holiday travelers, bright lights, and all the elegance of a four-star hotel. Fu Shuang was in sensory overload.

When they got to their room, she looked with amazement at the elegant decor, and the massive bed her parents indicated was hers. She had never slept in a bed so large. The beds at the orphanage were more like cots, tiny and thin. This one was downright luxurious, with a thick mattress, two fluffy pillows, a soft blanket, and clean linen that smelled to her like lavender tea. Despite its large size, she didn't have to share it with anyone: it was *her* bed. She did have to share the room with her new parents, though, and while she was used to sleeping with roommates, she wasn't used to sleeping with complete strangers. It felt odd.

Her parents gave her more gifts, including a personal CD player with earphones, which she tentatively put on. It was the first time she had listened to music in this manner, and she was transported. It was like being in a world of her own. The songs were sung in English, so she didn't understand the lyrics, but the tunes are catchy and enjoyable. Fu Shuang loved this new technology and tried to indicate her gratitude. Immediately she knew she'd be able to listen to music and tune out everything else, and this alone would make the awkward days ahead go by quickly and easily.

That night her parents took her to the fancy restaurant in the hotel. She liked going out to eat, and after a lifetime of never getting enough food, she appreciated that she was able to eat whatever she wanted, as much as she wanted, including soda and dessert. The food in the hotel was Chinese, and not only was she glad she didn't have to try to choke down another hamburger, it was some of the best food she had ever eaten.

While it was strange to be away from the orphanage, so far, she liked the advantages she was experiencing in this new life. *My fortunes are turning. Luck times two is at work. First, I was saved by my Nai Nai who brought me to the orphanage. Now, I'm adopted and going to America. I'm truly blessed.*

Back in the hotel room, Fu Shuang lay in her gigantic bed, dreaming of her friends and her life in Benxi. She knew that nothing would ever be the same and she would miss her orphanage and her beloved China, but a new life was dawning and she could already see that the sunrise was beautiful. Tomorrow, more paperwork and then, just like that, the adoption would be final. After that, there was no turning back.

# Chapter 13:
# The Big Day

## Sandi

It was the end of what I had been coming to think was endless paperwork. The official documents were completed, and the information that needed to be transferred from the US forms to the Chinese forms had been provided. Everything had been signed, notarized, and accepted by China. Most of the morning was spent getting this accomplished. We visited several different governmental buildings, answered what felt like hundreds of questions, and climbed into and out of about a dozen taxis. This was a major achievement as the traffic was insane, which was unfortunately matched by the driving style of the Chinese cabbies. But at the end of the day on September 27, 2004, it was final – Dang Fu Shuang became Sierra Fu Shuang Wilson, our daughter, and part of our family forever.

—

Adoption is a miracle.

Birth parents give up a child for many reasons. Often the child can't be properly cared for, accepted, or financially supported. Some birth parents simply don't have the emotional maturity to handle being responsible for another human being. There may be pressure from family or society to give up the child, as is the case in China with the one-child policy. For whatever reason, the child is surrendered to someone else, and there's no way to know if this will be a disaster, or the best thing that could have happened.

Sedona was fourteen months old when she joined our family. Since she was our first child, we were terribly nervous – and as it happened, we had every reason to be. Although she hadn't been diagnosed, we believe she came with reactive attachment disorder (RAD,) due to her lack of social interaction during early infancy. Our physician in Phoenix believed that Sedona had been left in her crib all day every day, so she didn't learn to crawl when most children do, and her leg muscles hadn't developed. She didn't like being held or talked to, probably because she had so many different caretakers as a baby, and she was unable, at first, to bond with anyone. Though we addressed these issues immediately, they took years to overcome. Sedona was beautiful, cerebral, and stubborn. She carried boxes of food around with her as soon as she was able to walk, fearing scarcity. We loved her with all our hearts, but the adjustment period was long and difficult for everyone. Even today she's frugal with her money and her things, as if worried there won't be more. I can't imagine what she experienced in the first fourteen months of her life, though I suspect she'll always carry the emotional baggage she picked up as an infant.

PJ was ten months old when we traveled to Guatemala to meet him. He had a serious physical defect called patent ductus arteriosus (PDA,) a congenital heart condition that involves a hole in the aorta. For most people who carry the genetic marker, the hole closes at birth so blood can circulate properly into the lungs, but in a few cases it doesn't, which creates the full-blown PDA condition. In Parker's case the hole didn't close. He was short of breath, had poor circulation, was often sick, and needed surgery immediately upon arrival in Phoenix. The cardiologist who performed his first heart procedure said it was the largest PDA hole he had ever seen or operated on. The first surgery was only partially successful, and we were told he'd need another surgery. He ended up having one additional surgery to fix the heart problem, and then two other unrelated operations, all before he was five. Despite so much time spent in hospitals, he was a smiling, happy little boy, joyful and well-connected to his new family. We loved him dearly.

—

The one thing we'd learned from two adoptions was that we couldn't predict how it would go with Sierra. We didn't know if she'd be able to adjust quickly, or if she'd be emotionally hampered by this abrupt and dramatic change in her life. She might have physical or emotional issues we didn't know about that would need to be addressed, either immediately or down the road. Since each child is an individual with his or her own specific needs, our previous experiences didn't give us any idea what to expect.

I worried about her. She seemed well adjusted and curious, but there was going to be a *lot* for her to learn. She would have to learn a new language, meet and become part of a whole new family, go to a new school, and discover who she would be in this new country. She'd also be dealing with the onset of puberty, which added extra challenges. I prayed she'd have the courage and fortitude to find her way. I had a feeling this tiny but determined young lady would handle everything life could throw at her, but we didn't know, and neither did she.

## Chapter 14: Becoming Sierra's Parents

### Sandi

We wanted Sierra to begin to understand family, since she'd never had one, and we thought the best way to do this was to be travelers in this wonderful land, being together as a family unit, making memories, in her element rather than ours. There was still some paperwork necessary to get Sierra home, but it was minor in comparison to what we'd already completed, so the adventure began.

Most of our time in China was spent touring monuments, temples, and picturesque gardens, and generally enjoying the countryside. To desert dwellers like Paul and me, the sheer abundance of greenery was glorious; all around us were rice fields and other agricultural crops, and a riot of natural vegetation. Sierra seemed enthralled with her ability to act like a tourist in her native home. Prior to this, she was stuck in either her orphanage or her boarding school, with little exposure to the wonders of China. Now, she was learning to be part of a family, and at the same time learning about her native land, having adventures, and making new memories. China is beautiful, but to us Sierra was even more beautiful, and becoming more so each moment as we got to know her.

On the first morning of our time together, we went down to the restaurant for breakfast. Again, we didn't know much about Sierra, or her morning ritual, and she didn't know about ours, but as we discovered she was eager to find out. Paul had coffee and I ordered tea. Sierra, wanting to be like her father, requested coffee as well. We thought this unusual for a twelve-year-old girl, but for all we knew, she'd had coffee every morning of her life. The drinks came and Paul put cream and sugar into his cup. I watched with fascination as Sierra followed suit. Then she took a sip. Her mouth twisted in a grimace, she spat the coffee back into her cup, and exclaimed something in Chinese we didn't understand but that sounded profane. Paul and I broke out in laughter, and she began laughing as well. Now we knew two more things about her: she wasn't a coffee drinker, and she had a sense of humor.

—

In addition to being sightseers, we were getting acquainted day by day. It didn't take me long to notice that Sierra had attached herself to her dad, quite literally. She clung to him like she was at sea and he was a life vest. It was adorable, but to be honest it also hurt. She wasn't interested in getting to know me at all, and even though I knew she needed to adjust, it was frustrating. I felt that I had *earned* a new daughter. I'd worked hard to get us to this point. I told myself things would change when we got home, this was just a temporary thing, and did my best to hide my disappointment. But every day she avoided me felt like a knife twisting in my heart, and I confess I cried myself to sleep more than once.

"Paul," I said one evening, "Why isn't Sierra bonding with me? I feel like I'm open and available to her, but she keeps pushing me away."

"You're trying too hard," he said. "You need to give her some space and let her find her own way. Let's be honest, you can be domineering. I'm guessing she senses that in you and it's intimidating."

This was hard to hear, but I was glad I could trust Paul to tell me the truth. I tried to back off, to let Sierra come to me. But she continued to keep me at arm's length during our tour of China, and for the first time it occurred to me that she might not *want* a mother. I wondered what effect that would have on our lives, if it was true.

# Chapter 15: Sierra's Plan

## Sierra

Fu Shuang – now Sierra – loved the freedom she'd acquired since leaving the orphanage. There was so much to see and do and experience. "Life is good," she said to one of the interpreters after a tour of a Buddhist temple, beaming.

Sierra quickly became comfortable with her new father, partially because of the great relationship she had with her Shu Shu – the orphanage administrator "uncle" who had taken such a liking to her when she was very small. Her Shu Shu had been kind and generous, and she felt instinctively she'd have a similar relationship with her new dad. He was also quick to smile and played ping-pong and basketball with her at the hotel gym. She loved being active, and this gave them a way to be together where their inability to converse wasn't a problem.

Her mother made her uncomfortable, though. Sierra had been surrounded by women in the orphanage, and some were harsh disciplinarians rather than nurturing caregivers. They had high expectations for the children and were focused on making them well behaved and obedient. Without any other adult female role models, Sierra assumed her new mother would be the same way, so while she could, she steered clear. There would be time enough to deal with the unpleasant parts of her family life when she got to America and into a regular routine. She wasn't about to ruin her freedom by getting to know a mother who would undoubtedly make her start earning her keep.

Her father didn't seem to mind her spending her time with him. In fact, she thought he was reveling in the attention. Sierra would continue to stick with her dad and hang back with her mom – though she would never go so far as to be rude. It seemed to be a good approach, as her new mother didn't push or insist on being involved.

This just might work.

—

One of Sierra's most memorable trips was the afternoon her parents took her shopping. She'd never been to a mall in her life and didn't even know what it was, or what to expect. But since the only clothes she had were the orphanage hand-me-downs she was wearing, she was going to need more clothes than the few her mother had brought from Phoenix.

The mall in Shenyang was sizable. The family's first stop was a large department store, which Sierra thought truly magnificent. She was wide-eyed as they walked among suites of furniture, stacks of appliances, shelves of home goods, and aisles of shoes and clothing. She was like a reluctant mule as she was dragged, eyes protruding, to the girls' department. Once there, she looked around in amazement, unable to believe her eyes. She saw racks of pants, shirts, skirts, and dresses of every type, pattern, shape, and size. There were shelves with underwear, socks, and accessories, and next to the girls' clothing was a whole department just for shoes. The array of colors was dazzling. Sierra's delight spread to her new parents as they watched her ecstatic reaction.

She'd been told she was going to get a couple of different outfits, so she picked out items in yellow, blue, and green, but red was clearly her "go-to" color. Mom and daughter stood in the fitting room as Sierra tried everything on, and the girl grinned at her reflection in the full-length mirror. She'd never seen herself in new clothes. She was used to hand-me-downs and faded, torn garments. Picking out new clothes that represented *her* personality and *her* desires was totally foreign, but she liked it.

In the end, she decided on a red Minnie Mouse sweatshirt with a large picture of a surprised and happy mouse on the front, and matching red sweatpants. Her second choice was tan pants and a bright yellow sweater that had the letters K-I-D printed vertically down the right side, outlined with metallic-looking beads. She practically strutted out of the store, carrying her bag of clothes and holding tightly onto her dad.

—

Sierra was amazed at the reaction she got from other Chinese people as she walked around Shenyang with her American parents. People stopped her at the hotel, in the street, and in restaurants, and asked her about the couple she was with. She explained that she was an orphan and that this was her new family, who had come from the United States to get her. People smiled to know she was being adopted, and even gave her thumbs-up signals. Many had never seen or interacted with Americans before, so they asked to take a picture of the family so they could remember the occasion. Sierra thought it was odd, but it was also kind of nice to be the focus of so much positive attention.

Sierra herself took a lot of pictures, to help her remember China. She loved her camera almost as much as her personal CD player and was always listening to music and taking pictures. She was amazed at how big everything seemed to be in China, and how much there was to see. She was learning more about her own country in this time with her new family than she'd ever learned through history books at boarding school.

The last city they visited was Guangzhou, and it was a wonderful experience for Sierra. There are many different Chinese dialects, the main ones being Mandarin and Cantonese. But while they're referred to as dialects, they're so dissimilar they could be completely different languages – people who speak Mandarin can't understand Cantonese speakers, and vice versa.

The residents of Guangzhou speak Cantonese; Sierra spoke Mandarin.

But somehow, she was still able to communicate roughly. She talked with everyone she saw and made friends in every shop and restaurant, and if she had trouble conveying information, she'd just keep at it until she got her point across. They'd leave for America from Guangzhou, and Sierra enjoyed every minute of her time in their exit city.

## Chapter 16:
# A China to Remember

### Sandi

One afternoon in Shenyang we went to a place called Zhongshan Park, just half a mile from the hotel. The weather seemed pleasant, though humid, and we walked from the hotel to the park. There was a festival going on in the park, with entertainment and food, and people everywhere. We stopped to have some lunch and Sierra ordered sausage on a bun, which she scarfed down quickly. We had learned something new about her – she loved sausage. We were getting to know her as she was getting to know us.

As we walked around the busy festival, where the Mandarin language flowed and happy children ran in every direction, we felt like a family. The sky had turned cloudy, but the festival was in full swing, and colorful flags beckoned everyone to join the fun. There were vendors selling all kinds of wares and we decided to buy Sierra a bracelet. She obviously wasn't used to receiving gifts, and apart from the watch we'd sent her, I doubted she'd ever owned any jewelry. We let her pick the bracelet out herself, and she chose a small one with polished brown and black beads of various sizes on an elastic band – just an inexpensive little trinket. But as we left the stall, she held onto it like it was a fourteen-karat treasure.

Next we stopped at a large stage to watch a show with clowns and juggling. Two of the clowns looked familiar, and I said as much to Paul.

He agreed. "I think we've seen them in Phoenix."

The female clown sported a blue, shoulder-length wig and when she looked in my direction, she nodded in recognition. But before I could marvel over meeting someone I knew here, in the vastness of China, the skies opened. The rest of the audience ran for cover, but we hadn't brought an umbrella and had nowhere to go. We stood there, getting soaked as we looked around for somewhere to take shelter, when I felt a tap on my shoulder. I turned to see the clown with the blue wig.

"Hi, don't I know you?" she said in American-accented English.

"We were just saying you looked familiar," I said. "I think we've seen you at Macayo's Restaurant in Phoenix. Don't you make balloons for the kids?"

"I do. Why don't you follow me backstage and get out of the weather?"

As we waited for the rain to let up, we exchanged introductions with our hosts. The blue-haired clown's name was Bethany, and she explained that she and her husband, who was also a clown, did six-month stints in China to make extra money. They were in Shenyang for a couple more months before they would return to Phoenix. We chatted about how remarkable it was that we were in China at the same time, and we explained about Sierra's adoption. When the weather cleared enough for us to go, they lent us their umbrella and we promised to drop it off at their hotel the next day. The smallness of the world had just been proven to us.

One afternoon, a young college student who was also our local interpreter escorted us around Beiling Park, noted for its stunning examples of Chinese architecture. The park was established in 1927 and included the tomb of the second Qing emperor, Huang Taji. The tomb, built between 1643 and 1651, was a traditional two-tier Chinese structure with red walls and an orange tile roof. In front of the tomb stood a giant gray concrete statue of Huang Taji. The emperor was positioned on a beige podium, displayed as a military leader with sword, traditional Chinese uniform, cape, and helmet with an arrow on top. We happened to be there during a military exhibition, and while Paul and I weren't sure what was happening, Sierra stood at attention. Her patriotism showed as she stood erect and saluted the passing solders as they marched by. The soldiers were unsmiling and stoic in olive-green uniforms with red scarves around their necks. They marched much like the films I remember from Nazi Germany during World War II, with straight legs. It all felt very strange and very communist, and I found it a little unnerving. But despite my unease, it was great to see Sierra's respect for her homeland.

Before we left Shenyang, we took a trip back to Sierra's orphanage in Benxi. The trip to Benxi was different from anything else I'd experienced in China. It was a rural area and the road was unpaved, so it was a bumpy ride. There were bicycles with Chinese wagons behind them, some filled with caged live chickens. I saw an ox pulling a rickshaw led by a wrinkled, dark-skinned man. Trucks were filled with produce: corn, apples, and all sorts of vegetables and herbs. There were rows and rows of cornfields, and cows and chickens roamed freely. It was as if we'd been transported back in time to another century.

When we arrived at the orphanage, I was surprised at the beauty of the buildings. Right across the street from the main building was an attractive little park with a playground and a small pond with a concrete bridge. It was quite serene and picturesque.

But once inside the main orphanage building, I was startled to see the furnishings were quite stark. While the rooms were clean, they were also simple and downright Spartan in appearance and functionality. It was apparent that the orphanage was operating on a shoestring and that the funding for the institution was modest.

Paul and I had the privilege of talking with the orphanage director and staff and learned a little more about Sierra. They said she was a carefree child who was loved by everyone, especially the other children. She was helpful and jovial every day. They were so happy that she had been adopted, and so grateful that we had agreed to come to their facility so she could say her final goodbyes.

The orphanage officials made us an extravagant lunch and we felt like important dignitaries. As we got close to the dining room, the smell of ginger, soy sauce, and exotic Asian spices filled the air. We were seated at a table with a lazy Susan in the middle, filled with delectable food. Halfway through the meal my stomach was bursting, but the dishes kept coming. Some of them were vaguely familiar, but it wasn't the American-Chinese food we had at restaurants in Phoenix, and much of it we didn't recognize at all. I tried most of the dishes, which were delicious, but stayed away from the pig's feet. I wasn't feeling *that* adventurous.

While Sierra could have eaten at the table with us, she decided to eat in the kitchen with the younger children, so she could say her goodbyes for the last time. It was a great opportunity to see her in her element, and it was obvious she felt tremendous affection for these preschoolers. Before we left, she gave them candy that we'd picked up in Shenyang. The orphans' faces lit up as they received their sweets, but Sierra's shone with joy at being able to share the small gift with her young friends.

Once we left Shenyang, we flew to Guangzhou. It was the first time Sierra had been on an airplane and she looked around the airport with amazed eyes, talking to everyone as we waited for our flight. Her gregarious good cheer seemed contagious, as people almost always responded to her with smiles and chatter of their own. Once we were on the plane, Sierra gazed out the window during the entire flight, content to stare at the clouds below, delight and amazement on her face.

Guangzhou is the exit point for all international travelers who adopt from China. You must go through this port to finalize the paperwork for the US Immigration and Naturalization Service, and have the paperwork checked by the American Embassy and the State Department. We were back to bureaucracy and administrative functions.

One of the important elements on this leg of the trip was to ensure that Sierra had all the required immunizations. The State Department requires meticulous medical records, which weren't available in Sierra's case. The orphanage said she probably had most of the necessary shots, but the records simply weren't accessible, so our little Sierra endured a day filled with injections. I think the poor thing had over ten shots that day.

While in Guangzhou we stayed at the White Swan Hotel, a five-star resort. This is truly the most elegant and beautiful hotel I've ever lodged in. It was spectacular in size, splendor, and sophistication, and even housed a mall with shops selling art, jewelry, souvenirs, and more. Room service provided American, Chinese, and Italian food. In the middle of the lobby was an enormous koi pond fed by a waterfall and surrounded by lush tropical plants. The fish were orange, yellow-gold, red, white, and black – the colors of fallen leaves, transformed into scaly fish bodies.

There were six other families there who were adopting with the same agency we used. We all met up in Guangzhou and together we went to a few tourist attractions while completing our final administrative tasks. Like an extended family, we walked together, talked about our beautiful children, and celebrated our good fortune.

We discovered one of Sierra's greatest joys during this time with the other adoptive families. Most of them had babies or toddlers, and Sierra found that she could be of great assistance to these new parents. She was used to taking care of little ones at the orphanage, and it was something she was happy to do. She loved children and they loved her. She could make a cranky baby smile or stop a toddler from fussing, and the adoptive families with small children began to depend on her for help even though she couldn't communicate with them. She became a favorite in our group, and she reveled in her ability to make new friends. Paul and I began to see that Sierra had a knack with people.

The families went to the Six Banyan Tree Temple, the Chimelong Xiangjiang Safari Park, Sacred Heart Cathedral, and the Chen Family Temple. Of all of these, Sierra was most uncomfortable at the Safari Park. She didn't seem to appreciate the animals and avoided looking at them. This surprised us, as Sedona and PJ loved to go to the zoo. The park had pandas, which was a treat for Paul and me, but they didn't seem to register any importance to Sierra. We wondered if this was because she'd never been around animals at the orphanage, if it was a personal thing, or if she was simply too exhausted to care. We'd been having a wonderful time in China, but we were all tired.

We had one more day in Guangzhou and then we would fly back to Phoenix. Sierra would meet her sister and brother, her grandmother and aunts and uncles and cousins, and her new life would begin. We didn't know if we'd ever return to China, so on our last day we walked around and tried to take it all in. We soaked up the sight of the currant-colored bricks and crimson trim and opened our ears to the harsh lilt of the Cantonese dialect around us. We reveled in the serenity of the plush green gardens, with their placid ponds and lotus flowers of every hue. We wandered the busy streets and shopped in the small pedestrian pathways. We immersed ourselves in the scrumptious smells of the food, and we smiled at the friendly faces. This was China, with its ancient culture and traditions, rubbing elbows with the modern world. We would miss China forever.

# Chapter 17: Phoenix Life

## Sedona and PJ

While we were in China, we got regular updates on the well-being of our children. Paul and I didn't like to be away from the kids and we rarely had occasion to leave them. We'd spent thirteen years without children, which had been plenty, so we were all about maximizing family moments. Most of the time everyone was happy with this arrangement, but it did mean Sedona and PJ were unprepared for two and a half weeks without their mom and dad.

Grandma and my friend Andree, Sedona's godmother, were assigned the challenging duty of babysitting. Sedona was wonderfully self-sufficient, but she was also used to getting her way. Stubborn and direct, she became a real test for the patience of her grandmother and godmother. She constantly told them the correct way to do everything, from feeding the animals to cooking meals. Her grandmother was fairly used to this, but Andree was surprised at Sedona's directness. "She's judge and jury, but also a helpful observer when you really do require assistance," Andree told me later.

While Sedona was fine staying home with G-ma and Andy, as she called them, PJ missed his parents terribly. Like many children his age, he loved routine. Change didn't come easy to him. The schedule he preferred on nonschool days was: up at dawn, a simple breakfast while watching TV, play until lunch, then a nap, followed by coloring or a game of hide-and-seek if he could coax anyone into playing. Finally, dinner, bath, a story, prayers, and bed. A full, rich day when you're four years old.

Sunrise in Phoenix occurs between 6:00 and 6:30 in autumn, and PJ and Sedona were up as the sky streaked with rose and orange, before the bright Arizona sun was even over the horizon. Neither Andree nor my mom was an early riser, which was distressing to PJ.

"Grandma get up and play," PJ said plaintively each Saturday and Sunday morning, ready to be unhappy that his schedule was disrupted. Luckily, Sedona was glad to assume her role as big sister and surrogate mom, so she'd maneuver him downstairs, get him breakfast, and turn on *Thomas the Tank Engine* for him. By the time Andy and G-ma were up, PJ was already busy with the day, thanks to Sedona.

During the work week, the kids' routine had the predictability PJ was looking for. They got up, ate breakfast, got dressed, and went to school. Andree had the job of getting them to their destinations. Dropping Sedona off from the carpool lane at St. John Bosco was simple; she hopped out and went into the school without fuss or fanfare. But when Andree drove PJ to Desert Garden Montessori, his exit from the car was the opposite of Sedona's. Andree was obliged to take his hand and lead him into the school as he became increasingly sad. While he liked the predictability of preschool and generally had a good time, he would cry whenever she left him there. This was heartbreaking for Andree and reminded her of her own son when he was a toddler. PJ was having a difficult time without his parents.

Before we left for China, one of my dear friends, Kerstin, and her husband Carl agreed to take the kids for one day to give Mom and Andree a bit of a break. Kerstin and Carl, adoptive parents as well, had a daughter, Julia, who was a friend of Sedona's. They had been to our house and we had been to theirs, so we knew Sedona would love a day with her friend and we hoped PJ would be okay spending time with them, since he knew them well. PJ could be difficult with food, and I had let Kerstin know about his picky palate so it wouldn't come as a surprise. At the time, he wouldn't eat vegetables and liked only very bland food. Kerstin informed me that she would get PJ to eat whatever she put in front of him. I just laughed, knowing, as only a mother can know, what she was in for if he was unhappy with the menu.

When the day came for them to go with Kerstin and Carl, the kids were especially excited because they were going to the circus. All three kids had a wonderful time. They were delighted by the animals and riveted by the high-wire acts and acrobats. The day flew by in a whirlwind of sights, sounds, and smells, and they returned to Kerstin and Carl's home tired but happy, to play and eat dinner.

Kerstin prepared meat, rice, and carrots. She fixed plates for everyone and set them in front of each kid. Sedona and Julia began eating without complaint, but PJ just scowled at the food. The meat and rice were acceptable to him, but *there was something orange on his plate*, and he thought it smelled foul.

"I'm not eating the veggie stuff. It smells icky and it's making my tummy sick," PJ said.

"You have to try everything on your plate," Kerstin said. "The orange stuff is good for you."

Dinner went on and PJ ate around the cooked carrots, silently picking at his food, not joining the girls' conversation about the circus. Worry filled his little face. Finally, everything was gone except for the veggies and he looked at Kerstin with tears in his eyes. "Do I have to eat them?" he asked.

"Yes, you do," she said, gently but firmly. "Just have a couple. They're really yummy, and really good for you."

PJ picked up his fork and placed one small carrot in his mouth. His face turned sour and he began to gag. Kerstin told him to swallow the food with a drink of water, which he did. Then it happened – everything came back up and landed right back on his plate as a revolting burnt orange mush. PJ began to sob, and Sedona got up and led him to the bathroom to clean him up. Kerstin cleared the table and made a note to tell me that I was right, he just wouldn't eat vegetables.

—

We called PJ and Sedona about every third day while we were gone, to hear their voices and to touch base with Andree and Mom. The kids were counting the days until our return, anxious to see us again and excited to meet their new sister. They couldn't speak with Sierra because of the language obstacle, but they were thrilled to hear about her. On the last phone call before our return home, Sedona exclaimed that she would show Sierra around and be her guide. It was reassuring to know she hadn't changed her mind, and that Sierra would be welcomed by her new siblings.

# Chapter 18: The Family Unit

## Sandi

After a long, long flight, we arrived at Sky Harbor, the Phoenix airport. We were greeted by Sonja from Hand-in-Hand and Brian, one of our best friends. PJ and Sedona called him Uncle Brian because he was so close and dear to our family. We were wiped out, but so grateful to be home and to see familiar faces. Sonja and Brian both gave us huge hugs as soon as they saw us. Sierra didn't know these folks, but she gave them a bright smile. She skipped as we left the airport, still holding on tightly to her dad, without regard or concern for me. Sonja, who was observant and knew me well at this point, noticed and mentioned it to me then and there. I admitted my fears to her that Sierra's relationship with me was somehow flawed before it had even started. She looked thoughtful but didn't comment further. I knew that if I needed her guidance, she would counsel me.

It was night in early October, and about ninety degrees out. This wasn't unusual for Phoenix but did seem to surprise Sierra. Brian drove us the fifteen miles from Sky Harbor to our home and Sierra stared, wide-eyed, out the window the whole way. I can't even imagine how exotic our very modern desert city was for her. We live in an area of Phoenix called Ahwatukee, which is south of downtown Phoenix and the airport, near South Mountain. When we got home, Brian helped us carry in our luggage, but didn't stay.

Sierra and Sedona were so excited to meet each other after all this buildup that the two girls started jumping all over the furniture and tearing around the house like a pair of hyenas. Thanks to their hysterical giggling – we knew they were exhausted – they sounded like hyenas, too. Mom and Andree looked at each other and decided to leave us with our new family. My mom would later tell me she was appalled by the girls' behavior and our lack of discipline with them, but frankly, we were too tired to deal with it. We were also so delighted to be home with Sierra at long last that we didn't want to immediately start being disciplinarians. We watched the girls' frenzied play with smiles on our faces.

PJ was already asleep. It was a difficult call, since I knew my sweet boy needed his rest, but this was an important moment for the family, and I decided to wake him up. He was excited to meet Sierra, but quickly fell back into slumber. He was like a puppy who wakes up, wags his tail, plays for a moment, then dozes off again where he sits. PJ would meet his new sister properly in the morning.

We showed Sierra around the house, and the look on her face is still vivid in my memory. She was stunned to find that she had her own bedroom. Clearly, she hadn't expected or even imagined such luxury. When we somehow managed to convey that the room was all hers and she didn't have to share it with anyone, she was astonished and delighted. We had painted it pink and hung posters on the walls we thought an adolescent girl would like. Sedona had helped me pick out a pink and purple bedspread with glitter-enhanced butterflies, and it sparkled in the lamplight. The luminous smile on Sierra's drowsy face reflected her pleasure.

The challenging part of the night came when she met our cat. Barkley was a smoky gray Persian with a lion-cut mane around his face, a shaved body and tail, tufts of fur on the end of his tail and around his feet. Sierra physically recoiled when she met him, clearly frightened by his appearance. We realized she wasn't accustomed to being around pets but didn't expect a severe reaction. Barkley meowed quietly at her and began to purr, but this didn't help the situation. I don't think she'd ever been around a cat, and the strange rumbling noise Barkley was making caused more alarm. It was funny to us, but we didn't let it show, because he was a very peaceful feline.

It was way past time for three of us to get to bed, so we called it a night. I dropped into bed, too exhausted to worry about the future and how Sierra was going to fit with the rest of the Wilsons.

—

On the second day, Sierra was introduced to our family dog, Josie. She was a gentle soul, a big black Labrador Retriever who liked to carry rocks around in her mouth – we said that Josie was always packing. Sierra was as petrified of Josie as she had been of Barkley; she didn't even want to be in the same room with either of them. Because Sedona and PJ both adored their pets, they were very upset that Sierra didn't like them, and there was quite a bit of drama around this topic. Paul and I explained that she hadn't been around animals the way they had, and they tried to understand, but they couldn't imagine life without pets. It was one of the many adjustments the household had to make as Sierra became part of our crew. She avoided the animals and retreated whenever she saw them. We all had to respect this fear, and hope that over time she'd become more comfortable with the four-legged members of the tribe.

The next day Sierra saw her surroundings in full daylight for the first time. She explored her new home and seemed pleased by it. She also seemed to like having a sister and a brother, though the lack of shared language severely limited their ability to get to know each other. At one point when I wasn't in the room, some breakdown occurred among them that resulted in Sierra crying. To this day I don't know what happened, but it was an unpleasant event on her first full day home.

Sierra also saw her grandmother again on that second day, and met her Uncle Bob, Aunt Sheree, and cousins Kelsee and Joe. When she was introduced to her family, Sierra opened with "Hello. How are you? I am fine and thank you." Her facility with this phrase led the family to believe that she spoke English. Of course, she did not, and I explained that those three little sentences were the extent of her repertoire. This continued to happen whenever she met new people. She was so adept at those phrases. It was impressive, if confusing.

—

In the first weeks, my relationship with Sierra was my biggest concern. I knew she had to be overwhelmed by the changes in her life, and certainly her relationship with everyone in the family needed to solidify – I was just one of the cogs in the wheel. But the way she'd kept such a distance from me the whole time in China meant I already had extra ground to make up. I remembered what Paul had said and didn't push, but I felt like I was holding my breath as the days became weeks. I watched her carefully, made mental notes of her challenges, and tried to show care and attention without overwhelming her.

After a few very long weeks, it became apparent that whatever had been going on in China with our relationship, was *not* going to carry over to home. Sierra was still very close with her dad, but she finally seemed to be opening up to me too. She was holding onto any familiarity that she could muster, and in her new situation, I practically counted as an old acquaintance. Sierra was a brave girl, but changes were coming at her fast and she needed to be able to count on both her parents as she adjusted to her new surroundings. As she began to trust me the way she did Paul, I was finally able to exhale.

Next came doctor and dentist appointments, school enrollment, and the development of a routine. There was a lot of stressful driving around Phoenix. Because of our inability to converse, preparing her for an appointment was a chore. She never knew exactly what I wanted her to do, and it was extremely frustrating for us both. Activities that were easy with my younger kids, who knew the expectations, were just plain difficult with Sierra.

We went to her new primary care doctor and were referred to Phoenix Children's Hospital for a complete examination that would help us determine the issue with her back. Unfortunately, it would be a couple of months before we could get the appointments we needed.

Sierra was riding an emotional roller coaster, often from one minute to another. She had bought with her a DVD in China of a pop star she loved, and she watched it over and over. But it made her homesick, and she'd cry several times a day as she longed for China. She couldn't understand our language and we couldn't speak to her, and a depression began to descend on her. We could see that she tried to be content, and sometimes the brightness of her spirit peeked out from the corners of her eyes and her smile reunited with her face. But most days her emotions were raw and close to the surface.

Sierra also needed some serious dental work. Many of her baby teeth hadn't fallen out when they were supposed to, making it impossible for her permanent teeth to find a home in her tiny mouth. Over the next three weeks, she had eight baby teeth pulled, and the dentist told us she needed braces. Because there had been no room for them, her teeth were very crooked and needed to be straightened as soon as possible. This was not the greatest welcome to America for poor Sierra, but she took it like a champ. And though she continued to be sad, it was apparent that our new daughter had a beautiful, resilient spirit that couldn't be extinguished, no matter what obstacles she faced.

Our language barrier was somewhat bridged by my work friend, Nancy, who was originally from China and had come to America in adulthood, carrying with her a distinct Mandarin accent. She was an accountant in the Finance Department at Maricopa County, and a quiet, diligent, dedicated worker. When I asked her if she could help us talk to Sierra, she was eager to do whatever she could. Her pleasant face and genuine desire to help immediately put Sierra at ease, and Nancy became a godsend during the first several months. Whenever I had something to communicate and I couldn't get through to Sierra, I would call Nancy and she would translate for us. It worked in reverse as well. When Sierra wanted to tell me something, she would call Nancy, who would interpret. I'm not sure what would have happened if we hadn't had Nancy.

However, this exchange didn't always work as planned and it felt like we were playing the old "Telephone Game," where the first person whispers a phrase to the next person down the line and so on, and in the end the original phrase has somehow changed dramatically. This sometimes happened with our translations, and the result was always confusing, and usually funny. In addition, Nancy often found herself speaking Chinese to me or English to Sierra, and we'd all break out laughing. I think the laughter was almost as helpful in overcoming the language problem as the translations.

—

Sierra's first holiday in the United States was Halloween. This celebration was very alien to her. We tried to show her what the holiday was about, without much luck. Nancy spoke with Sierra and explained, but she didn't fare any better than we had. However, knowing how much Sedona and PJ loved the holiday, I was determined to ensure that Sierra fully experienced her first Halloween. We had four events to attend, so we went to the store to pick out costumes. Sierra chose a witch, though I don't think she knew what it was. It was an old-fashioned-looking black peasant dress with orange trim on the front and a ragged hem. She looked adorable, but she clearly had no idea why she was dressed this way. PJ decided to be a Teenage Mutant Ninja Turtle, and Sedona a cowgirl. When they all got decked out, the kids truly looked like siblings.

The first event was the annual neighborhood Halloween party. This was a block party and was the one day of the year when all the neighbors interacted with each other. There was plenty of candy and lots of games for the kids, and it was a great chance to introduce Sierra to our neighbors. Everyone was excited to meet the newest member of our family, and it was wonderful to feel like part of such a welcoming community. Because there were a lot of kids at the party, Sierra had a blast. She was not at all shy and participated in the games and events to the best of her ability. In one game, she partnered with her sister, and the girls threw a water balloon to each other, trying not to break the balloon as they moved farther apart with each toss. They won second place and a prize, which thrilled the sister team.

The second event was held at a local farm in Queen Creek, not far from our home. Schnepf Farms held an annual Pumpkin Festival and we tried to go every year. Sedona and PJ loved to pick out a pumpkin, ride the train and other rides at the small carnival, and go through the hay maze. This year, we went with two of Sedona's friends, Samantha and Lillian. It was a hot day, but the kids didn't seem to mind. PJ ran around, jumping up and down in excitement, and enjoying his time with all the girls. Except for his father, he was surrounded by females – which he loved. Sierra took him under her wing and watched him while Sedona ran off with her friends. Everyone loved the afternoon, and Sierra appeared to get into the Halloween spirit.

The third event was the St. John Bosco Fall Festival, an annual school fundraiser that Sedona and PJ treasured. It had a bouncy house, game booths, food and candy, and of course, a costume contest. Sierra still may not have understood what Halloween was about, but she had a wonderful time, especially with so many little kids around. We strolled the campus as a family unit, and she looked proud to be a Wilson.

Finally, the main event: trick or treat on Halloween night. If you think about it, this is a strange tradition. Why, exactly, do we send our children out into the night to beg candy from our neighbors? It probably made sense to someone when the holiday started, but in modern America I have no idea what it's about. All I knew was that PJ and Sedona loved it, so we hoped Sierra would too.

We started the night by carving the pumpkin. Our jack-o'-lantern was smiling, but he did have a bit of a sinister smirk on his round, lopsided face. The other decorations displayed in the yard included fake gravestones, an old witch that cackled when you walked by, and Russell Scarecrow. Sedona, PJ, and I had made Russell the year before by stuffing old jeans and a shirt with newspaper, and making a papier-mâché pumpkin for a head. He sat on the porch in a lounge chair. Sierra found all of this too strange and insisted on calling Nancy to discuss.

"Why are they cutting up a pumpkin?" she said.

Nancy said, "It is a tradition in America. I think they are warding off evil spirits. It isn't anything to worry about. It is an Autumn celebration, like the Moon Festival in China."

"Well, I don't care for it," she said.

Nancy's explanation didn't increase her excitement in the holiday, and it passed without much fanfare, but she did love seeing all the other children in their Halloween costumes, especially the little ones. And she didn't object to the candy. Halloween 2004 was concluded, and Sierra had celebrated her first American holiday.

# Chapter 19: A Desert Home

## Sierra

On the drive to her new home from the airport, Sierra could see, even in the darkness, how different the scenery was. The earth looked dry and dusty, and instead of the lush foliage she was used to, everywhere she looked were strange spiky plants and stark, thorny trees. She'd never seen a desert before, so the arid, barren landscape was surprising, even unsettling. But other things made up for this drastic change in her surroundings.

"I have my own bedroom," Sierra told Nancy on the phone a few days later. "It's really cool. I like the big pink house, too. It has a nice backyard with a pool. It's like living in a fancy hotel. I really am double-lucky."

What Sierra didn't like was most of the food. She was introduced to pizza, hamburgers, French fries, chicken fingers, macaroni and cheese, Mexican food, Italian food, various meats, baked and mashed potatoes, all kinds of veggies, salads, and soups. But due to her limited diet at the orphanage and the bad food at the boarding school, she was a picky eater, and sustained herself on pickles, ramen noodles, rice, a few vegetables, and bananas. Surprisingly, given what she'd learned about her first visit, she began to like McDonald's. It didn't take too long before she'd willingly eat chicken nuggets, fries, and a Coke; I think PJ and Sedona's influence made the difference on this front.

The family took trips to the Chinese market so Sierra could pick out her favorite foods. She wanted pig's feet, fish, dumplings, and a lot of Chinese snack foods. Andree had returned to her home in New Orleans and received an emergency call from Sierra's mom to get a recipe for pig's feet. Cooking pig's feet was new for the Wilson household, but Sierra loved it. She also loved chicken drumsticks and would devour every morsel of meat and cartilage off the bone. When she was done, it looked like the drumstick had been dipped in acid. She jealously guarded her Chinese food, which was funny because none of the rest of the family had any interest in eating it.

Like most kids, she didn't like trips to the doctor or dentist, especially when she had to get so many teeth pulled. It was extremely painful, and she couldn't understand why the Americans were doing this to her. Nancy had to explain that her baby teeth were in the way of her permanent teeth.

"But my mouth is so sore," she told Nancy. "I wish they'd just stop. In China everyone left my teeth alone and they were fine."

—

Slowly, Sierra began to settle into her new life. Her first American holiday, Halloween, was confusing. She liked the candy and parties, and meeting all the neighbors, but the rest of the holiday made no sense to her. Dressing up and walking around like someone else wasn't her thing, and she was afraid other holidays would be similarly bizarre – though she had heard about Christmas in China and thought that sounded more her speed. She didn't know when it was, but she looked forward to it.

Above all, Sierra loved PJ and Sedona. They were like the orphans in China she considered her siblings, only they actually were her brother and sister. There was no more pretending: this was her family for real.

Despite her affection for them, the fact that Sierra's family didn't speak her language was hard on her. Although she was surrounded by people, she felt like she was living in isolation, without friends or companionship. She missed the sights, sounds, smells, and tastes of China. The desert terrain was strange, she didn't like the food, and her inability to communicate made her lonely. Apart from her one Chinese DVD, even the music was alien, and this made her even more melancholy. Everything in America was just so ... *different*, and some days she regretted coming.

One major area of adjustment for Sierra was her relationship with her mother. Though she'd kept her distance in China, in Phoenix she began to spend time with her mom and try to be affectionate. Much later, when she could speak English, she told the story of what changed for her.

"I learned soon after I arrived that if I wanted to make any progress in my new life, I needed my mom," she said. "I watched Sedona and PJ and I realized who ran the household, did the shopping, and helped with the homework, and I knew I needed to get with the program. I also realized that this was my mom and she would care for me. My mom was nothing like the women caretakers in China and that fear was not something I needed to carry around at home."

After that discussion and the sting of the first chilly interactions, the emotional separation melted away like snow on a sunny spring day. Mom and daughter were united in the plan to develop a new family life.

Sierra's sense of isolation diminished greatly once she was introduced to Nancy. It felt so good for her to be able to talk to someone. From then on, whenever Sierra was feeling excluded or lonely, she'd call Nancy. They conversed regularly, not only to translate family messages, but simply to communicate. Sierra missed speaking her native tongue, and even apart from finally being able to just *chat*, Nancy was Sierra's tie to China. Sierra later said, "Nancy taught me that I could transition, as she did, and become American without losing my Chinese roots. It was very comforting."

Though it was overwhelming to meet so many new relatives, family friends, neighbors, and teachers, it was also wonderful to have so many kind people wishing her well. In addition to her Uncle Bob, Aunt Sheree, and cousins Joe and Kelsee, who lived in Phoenix, she met her Aunt Barbara and cousin Lisa from California. She got to know her G-ma Helen, and her parents' friends Andree and Brian, who were so close they were practically family too. Sierra had seen pictures of many of these people in the scrapbook her parents had sent to China. In one, Brian was posed with her grandmother (thirty-seven years his senior), and Sierra had assumed they were married. When she admitted she'd thought Brian was her grandfather, everyone laughed, including Sierra. Brian sported a beard, and later, when Sierra learned about Christmas, she started to call him Santa Claus.

She quickly grew attached to her new extended family, and even began to warm up to the furry, four-footed Wilsons. Sedona and PJ had kept up a nonstop campaign to get Sierra to understand and accept Barkley and Josie, which mostly involved teaching her how cats and dogs communicated. Sierra learned that Josie was sweet-natured, and that licking was a doggie version of kissing. She also learned that Barkley was showing her love when he leaned into her leg, and that purring was his way of saying he was happy. All of this was new information to Sierra, but as she began to understand how to read the animals' signals, she began to value their affection. She never would have guessed two of her new family members would be covered in fur, but they became a source of great joy to her.

Life became easier as the English language began to click. Her primary care doctor suggested that Sierra watch a lot of television, explaining that immersion in English was the best way to ensure comprehension, so Sierra spent many hours soaking up shows on the Disney Channel, Nickelodeon, and the Cartoon Channel. She was a quick study and by Christmas – only two months after her arrival – she began to understand English and speak in simple phrases. After that she progressed rapidly, and her English began to flow.

# Chapter 20: Doctors within Our Borders

Sandi

Sierra's back was a concern to Paul and me, and her primary care doctor. As soon after her arrival as we could get an appointment, we took her to Phoenix Children's Hospital for a bone survey. This includes imaging the entire skeletal system, and Sierra spent one whole day getting X-rayed. The doctors there were perplexed when they saw her back. With her history of clubbed feet and her small stature, they felt she might have a genetic condition, so they sent her DNA to Johns Hopkins University for testing. In the meantime, they speculated that her back curvature, based on Sierra's account of her injury, was at least partially a result of her breaking her tailbone in China.

Sierra also went to see a pediatric orthopedic surgeon and a back surgeon to find out if corrective surgery was advised or necessary. In both cases, the doctors said it wouldn't be needed, since she didn't have discomfort or pain. Back surgery is a serious undertaking and the outcome isn't always an improvement, so that was a huge relief. Sierra was self-conscious about her back, but she was also relieved that she didn't need surgery.

About a year after her DNA was sent to Johns Hopkins, a diagnosis came back. She had a very rare genetic condition called Spondylocarpotarsal Synostosis Syndrome. This disease is hereditary, caused by a gene mutation present but normally recessive in both parents. Fortunately, it's not life threatening, but it certainly explained many of the issues that Sierra experienced, including her short stature, curved pinky fingers, clubbed feet, and swayed back (hyper-lordosis.) Because of this condition, Sierra would also have to be diligent about monitoring her eyesight and hearing.

All adolescents worry about being different, but Sierra was *very* different from the children around her. She was extremely short, with pronounced curvature of her back and crooked teeth. She was adopted, part of a tri-racial family, a non-native English speaker, and she'd spent her whole life in an orphanage. All of that would be a lot for even an adult to handle, much less a preadolescent.

Luckily, Sierra was no ordinary girl.

# Chapter 21:
# School Time, Cool Time

## Sandi

From the beginning it was critical to get Sierra enrolled in school and learning English, if only so we wouldn't have to call poor Nancy so often. PJ was attending preschool at Desert Garden, where Sedona had gone before switching to SJB, and I had talked to the director of the program about the possibility of Sierra becoming the third Wilson to attend the school. It seemed like the logical choice for her, because they had the resources to give her the individual attention she'd need, and we'd decided to send her there even before we'd brought her back to Phoenix. It was expensive, but the atmosphere was perfect for acclimation to her new life.

Montessori schools have a philosophy of noncompetitive learning, and focus on multigrade education, diversity, personal motivation, and individuality. Desert Garden Montessori (DGM), founded in 1996, provided education from preschool through middle school. When we'd met with the school's educators prior to Sierra's arrival, they'd told us Sierra's educational plan would focus on socialization, conversational English, language comprehension, and basic reading and writing skills, and that the initial emphasis would be on letters and phonetics. She'd learn math too, but it would be secondary to English.

We also talked with the administrators of several other schools, but in the end, Paul and I decided the Montessori environment would be the best school for Sierra, at least to begin with. DGM was a great caring environment, and with PJ there we thought it would be an easier transition for Sierra. The school's director and founder, Shetal Walters, understood the enormous challenge we faced. With little to no English skills, the entire process would be strenuous for Sierra, her parents and siblings, and her teachers and school administrators. Ms. Walters accepted the challenge with empathy, and after Sierra had been attending only a short time, we knew we'd made the right choice. Everyone was welcoming and patient, Sierra was happy, and PJ loved that his big sister went to his school.

—

One day, after Sierra had been at DGM for about six months, PJ came home from school crying because an older child had been bullying him. This kid wasn't in PJ's class but sought him out on the playground, where he called PJ names and made fun of his clothes. PJ began to be afraid to go to school, which made me furious for him. Paul and I talked about how to handle the situation, but PJ didn't want us to intervene, and it made him cry even harder.

"I will handle it," Sierra said at the dinner table. Sierra still spoke somewhat hesitant English, but this pronouncement was direct, honest, and sincere, and it was exactly what PJ needed to hear. "Don't worry, Mom and Dad, I will talk with this kid. I won't be mean, but I will let him know that this needs to stop, now." We weren't at all sure about letting her take the reins in this situation, but PJ was okay with it, so we decided to trust her and if it didn't work, step in ourselves.

At school the next day, Sierra watched the playground during morning recess. PJ played with his friends but kept a watchful eye on the older boy and managed to avoid him. From watching PJ, Sierra now knew which boy was the bully, and she decided to confront him at afternoon recess.

When the time came, she walked quietly up to the mean kid, whose back was turned to her. Sierra was slightly taller than the other child, but she was five years older. She calmly tapped him on the shoulder. When he turned around, she said, "Do you know who I am?"

"No, why would I?" the boy said, full of swagger.

"I am Sierra, and my brother is PJ. I have heard that you have been mean to my brother."

"What? Where did you hear that?"

"My brother told me. I do not wish this to be a problem, but I will be watching, and you will not come near him again.

I will tell the teachers and make this an issue if I see or hear that you have been mean to him or anyone else. Please be kind and don't bully the little kids. I may not be the biggest or strongest girl in the school, but I am not afraid of you. Please do not make me have to talk to you again. You will not like it."

The bully didn't respond, just scowled and stomped away. But the bullying abruptly stopped, and Sierra became a hero in her brother's eyes.

—

We had a daily routine for getting the kids to and from school: I dropped them off in the morning, and Paul picked them up after work. One day we got our wires crossed. Paul had a dentist appointment after work, so I was to oversee both drop-off and pick-up. But my own hectic day had scattered my brain and I completely forgot the plan. DGM closed its doors at 6:00 p.m., and at 5:45 p.m. I got a call from the school.

"Mrs. Wilson? PJ and Sierra are still at school. Is someone coming to get them?"

"What?" I said. "Paul hasn't picked them up yet?" Then I remembered *I* was supposed to have picked them up. I couldn't believe I'd forgotten my kids. I had to reboot my brain after I hung up. I frantically called Paul and we agreed that he would pick up Sedona at SJB, and I would get Sierra and PJ at DGM. I don't think I've ever driven so fast, or so unsafely, but I got there in record time, full of guilt and apologies.

Sierra confided later that she was afraid we'd changed our minds about keeping her and were leaving her at the school. I, of course, felt even more guilty after that confession. (And never again forgot to pick the kids up if it was my turn.) She also told me of a dream she had about taking a trip back to China. In the dream, the entire Wilson clan went to China for a vacation. We dropped Sierra off at her orphanage to visit with the children and caretakers, while the rest of us went on a tour of Benxi, planning to return in several hours. However, days later Sierra was still at the orphanage and we hadn't returned. The caretakers told her that her family had changed their minds, and Sierra would be staying at the orphanage instead of going back to America. When Sierra told me about this nightmare, I tried to reassure her that we would *never* leave her behind, that she was part of our family and would be forever, but she continued to be haunted by such fears for a long time.

# Chapter 22: American Girl

## Sierra

Talkative and outgoing by nature, Sierra was anxious to get back to communicating with others. The isolation created by the language gap was depressing. When she couldn't converse, she became lifeless, like a flower wilting without water. She wanted to be her confident and extroverted self, like she had been in China. Besides, she knew there were other things for her to learn, and to achieve them she needed to improve her language skills. Learning English was the key.

Desert Garden Montessori was a great fit for Sierra. The school was warm, inviting, and diverse. There were kids of all ages from babies to teens, which reminded her of the orphanage. The children were of all races and colors, from pale, red-haired kids to brown-skinned, black-haired children. In China, everyone was Asian, but this American diversity was something she immediately embraced, and thought was fabulous. The acceptance of everyone's differences was a universal trait at DGM, and it gave Sierra great comfort as she realized that she didn't have to look like her parents to be acknowledged or valued.

Sierra threw herself into conversational English, determined to be able to talk to people as quickly as possible. She received one-on-one lessons with several of the teachers throughout the day and practiced with flash cards to learn the names of objects. One week they might concentrate on kitchen items (stove, sink, refrigerator, oven, dishes, cups, forks, spoons, knives ...); the next week it might be animals. These exercises, and the dedication of teachers and students alike, not only helped Sierra learn English, but did wonders for her interpersonal skills.

In fact, she soon made good friends with two other preteen girls in her class – Chelsey and Justine. Although it was still difficult to communicate with them, the girls were content to show Sierra around the school and simply spend time with her. They were almost like bodyguards, as one or both could always be seen with her whenever they were on school grounds.

Through Nancy, Sierra told her mom that being part of the school and having friends had improved her outlook tremendously. She was meeting new people, learning to communicate with others, and having a good time with her classmates

– and she loved being known as PJ's big sister. As the school year progressed and her mastery of the English language increased, she began conversing and joking with most of the kids, and it wasn't long before she'd made many friends, of all ages. She started to lose her sense of isolation.

Phoenix was beginning to be home.

—

Another challenge Sierra faced in acclimating to American life was picking out clothes. First, there was the vast difference in style between China and the United States; second, at four feet, five inches, Sierra was short even by Chinese standards; third, like other girls her age, she was beginning to develop a more womanly figure; and fourth, at the orphanage she wore whatever fit her, which was often designed for much younger children. Because of all these issues, finding her properly fitting preteen clothing that she liked, could be quite difficult.

While her family wanted her to express herself, they didn't want her to be bullied or ridiculed for her clothing, so everyone tried to help her dress in a way that would allow her to be part of the crowd. One morning she emerged dressed for school with socks and sandals on her feet. Without words, her mom tried to explain that this was *not* going to fly with the other students, even at a school as accepting as DGM. Acting this out was so humurous that everyone laughed, but Sierra was still confused. Finally, her mother put on her own socks and sandals, and then took off her socks and put her sandals back on. Sierra watched with interest, and though the look on her face said she didn't understand what was wrong with wearing the two together, she got the point and took off her socks.

Sierra needed to find a style all her own and it developed over the first year. She loved neon colors, loose clothes, bling, and inspirational sayings. These all made their way into her wardrobe. However, in the beginning, her style choices were spotty as she didn't know what was "cool." She picked clothing based on what she was familiar with from China. No matter what she picked out, though, one thing was evident: she was a tomboy and she didn't want girly clothes.

On one of her shopping outings with her mom, Sierra saw some "Lizzy Maguire" athletic shoes – the kind that light up when they're in motion, usually worn by younger children. But Sierra had to have them.

"I love Lizzie Maguire! Please, Mom! I need those shoes!"

Finding a size that would fit Sierra's feet, which were indeed small, just not *toddler* small, was a monumental task that involved driving all over the Phoenix metropolitan area. By the ninth shoe store, her mom was sick of traffic and tried to convince her daughter she could survive without light-up Lizzie Maguire shoes, but Sierra begged her not to give up and – miracle of miracles –at the tenth store they found the right size.

Sierra was thrilled. Now her shoes shone as brightly as her personality.

As it turned out, she not only liked her clothes to be not only comfortable, but downright baggy. She discovered athletic shorts one day when the family was in the boys' department shopping for PJ. These were basketball shorts, shapeless and long, reaching the tops of her knees, and absolutely nothing like the shorts displayed in the girls' section.

"Mom, I want these shorts," she said. "They're comfortable and I like the length."

"But these aren't girls' shorts, Sierra," Mom said. "These are meant for young men. I think you should go back to the girls' section. I'm sure we can find you some shorts that are long and comfortable but designed for girls."

They tracked back to the girls' department and took another look around. Most of the options they found were short-shorts, or too girly, or snug-fitting, or all three. Those that weren't looked somehow out of proportion on her tiny frame.

Sierra insisted she wanted the other shorts, and although her mom thought it was an odd choice, in the end she had boys' basketball shorts in every color of the rainbow, though she had to tie the drawstring tightly to keep them on her slim body.

When Sierra finished developing her initial personal fashion sense, there was no doubt she had her own style. At four feet, five inches tall, with long, straight, jet-black hair, bling around her neck and in her ears, neon-colored shirts, light-up Lizzie Maguire tennis shoes, and baggy boys' shorts, she was a sight to behold.

As time went on, friends and family tried to encourage a little more convention with her clothes. Her grandmother talked with her about wearing dresses or slimmer fitting shorts and pants, but Sierra didn't agree and continued to wear her chosen attire with pride. Loved ones who were anxious to help her fit in a little more gave her dresses, jeans, and her first purse, but she rejected most of them. The purse was definitely not happening; she had a huge aversion to carrying one and simply wouldn't do it. This sometimes created tension between Sierra and well-meaning, caring adults. However, her independence won out.

Fortunately, her quirky personal style was accepted by her classmates in general, until she gradually became more American in her dress.

—

Sierra loved to play soccer, basketball, and baseball. She was determined to try all the sports and to be on as many athletic teams as she could fit into her schedule. She didn't know much about the rules of these games to start with and she wasn't a particularly great athlete, but she wasn't afraid to learn, and her enthusiasm was a plus for any team she joined.

Despite her love of team sports, she didn't need the approval of her peers. Many of the girls were boy-crazy, but this simply wasn't a part of her experience and she was uncomfortable with the idea of a boyfriend. In fact, she had trouble becoming close with any of the kids, girls or boys. She preferred to be part of a bigger group of friends, like she'd had at the orphanage. She wasn't a loner, but she wasn't dependent on any one person. Her happiness was generated from within.

She had a great desire for family, though. All her time in the orphanage she'd lacked a family connection, and now that she had it, family came first. Before she ever made plans with friends, she would find out if the family had plans, and would pass up a party with her classmates in favor of going to a movie with her mom and dad, brother and sister. Her parents were surprised by this lack of typical preteen behavior, but they were happy to have her stick so close to home.

# Chapter 23: Merry Winter Days

## Sandi

Christmas 2004 was special. Sierra hadn't celebrated Christmas before and really didn't understand what it was about. I asked Nancy to talk to Sierra about the various ways the holiday was celebrated, because I had tried to explain but clearly wasn't getting through. She was particularly confused about how Baby Jesus and Santa Claus were related. But even without understanding the nuances, she delighted in the hymns we sang in church and she loved Christmas music in general, so I began playing Christmas music in the car and the house all the time. Sierra also played it continuously on her iPod – I could hear it emanating from her earbuds as if it was an extension of her being. She learned about holiday traditions like baking, Christmas food and treats, decorating the tree and the house with bright colored lights, giving presents, and plenty of her favorite thing: family time.

When we asked Sierra what she wanted for Christmas, the list was long. She studied Toys R Us ads in the newspaper and marked everything she wanted. Because she hadn't enjoyed a typical American childhood, she wanted a lot of things that were meant for a much younger child – such as a baby doll and stroller, and clothes for the doll – but Paul and I got them for her anyway, thinking *better late than never*.

Sedona was surprised with Sierra's wish list. Sedona, seven years old at the time, wanted Gameboy video games, movies, CDs, stuffed animals, baseball cards, and clothes. Sedona was discovering that she was, in some ways, older than her big sister. Sedona and I talked about this, and the fact that it was Sierra's first Christmas. We discussed how the orphanage hadn't been able to supply the children with many material items, so Sierra hadn't experienced an abundance of toys when she was growing up. In fact, she hadn't personally owned anything. After our discussion, Sedona realized she had a lot to teach Sierra when it came to Christmas, and she liked that role. In this at least, she'd be Sierra's big sister as well as PJ's.

PJ himself was really beginning to understand the concept of Christmas and was thrilled. He wanted trucks and cars, Legos, Nerf guns, and superhero action figures. He wanted to see Santa and so did Sedona and Sierra, so we took them to the mall and got a Santa picture with all three kids. The joy on their faces was precious and this picture is still one of my very favorite Christmas photos.

I'm not sure when it started, but Paul and I had been sharing Christmas Eve with Brian since before we had kids. It had become our family tradition to attend mass with Uncle Brian, go to dinner at Red Lobster, then go home to exchange gifts, and we saw no reason to do things differently that year. We wanted Sierra to experience the full Wilson family Christmas.

Mass was beautiful. The church was exquisitely decorated with a large evergreen trimmed with white lights and a simple star, the Holy family prominently displayed behind the altar. A sense of tranquility pervaded the building, and the congregation radiated happiness. The hymns and carols got us in the holiday spirit, and we all sang "Joy to the World" on the way out of church. After dinner we went back to the house, where as far as the kids were concerned, Christmas Day had officially begun.

"Time to go to bed," I said to all three.

"We're too excited to go to bed," Sedona said, bouncing around the room to demonstrate.

"You have to get to bed and go to sleep," Paul said. "If you're not asleep by the time Santa gets here, he'll skip our house and you won't get any presents."

That was enough for PJ. "I'm going now. I'm tired."

But Sierra was confused. "I don't understand," she said. "Why won't he stop if we are awake? I was hoping to meet him. I didn't get a chance to really talk to him at the mall. I would like him to explain some things to me, like how he travels all over the world in one night, and why he doesn't visit China."

"He can't stop to chitchat," I said. "He has too much traveling to do." Sierra didn't look completely convinced, and I thought it wouldn't be long before her belief in Santa began to dissipate. But for now, I was happy she was able to believe for her first Christmas. I thought Sedona might already know the Santa secret, but if she did, she was keeping it quiet. They all scurried off to bed without further argument.

Brian always spent Christmas Eve with us after the kids went to bed. He helped Paul put together the toys that required assembly, which was always a significant job. Brian didn't have any kids of his own, so helping us get everything ready for the next morning was special for him – as well as for us. We would have been up for many, many hours without his assistance. Thank God for special friends like him.

The kids woke up before the break of dawn. PJ was the first to open his eyes and come in to get us up, but Sierra and Sedona were close behind. Paul went downstairs first to set up the video camera so we could capture the Christmas morning excitement. Then I took them down all at once to see what Santa had brought. In our house, Santa doesn't wrap his gifts, he just puts them under the tree, so they spotted their gifts and overstuffed stockings from Santa immediately. The kids exclaimed with pleasure as they investigated the haul. There was a note from Santa for PJ and Sedona that said he was proud of them for working hard at school and behaving for their parents in the past year, and a special note for Sierra saying how glad he was she had joined the Wilson clan, and that he had brought her an extra gift to make up for her years in the orphanage.

My mom, and Bob and his family, came over around eleven for our Christmas brunch and the family gift exchange. We had ham, scalloped potatoes, tamales, deviled eggs, chili cheese, green beans, a variety of salads, and lots of desserts. This feast reminded Sierra of Chinese New Year's, and she was in heaven. Sierra was beginning to enjoy American food, especially my mom's deviled eggs, and it was good to see her eat. She also enjoyed Bob's special poppy seed and nut rolls. This was a ritual that went back to my father. My dad had been a baker, of sorts, and this was a tradition that began with his Polish immigrant family. My paternal grandparents were born in Poland and immigrated to the United States as young adults. I was glad that Sierra was sharing this custom and loving the Polish sweet rolls.

We spent hours opening gifts, playing with the kids' toys, and catching up with each other's news. Our daily lives were crammed with work and obligations and we didn't get to see each other as much as we'd like. It felt good to slow down and visit.

But even though our traditions were the same each year, this year with Sierra changed the dynamics. There was a different type of Christmas spirit the newest Wilson brought to the festivities. Here was a child of twelve who believed in Santa and brought a real sense of wonder to Christmas. Sierra's delight in the holiday was infectious.

Unlike Halloween, Christmas was a tradition that she was glad to adopt. Christmas would always remain her favorite holiday and forever be a special family celebration.

# Chapter 24: Holidays in China and America

Sierra

Chinese New Year at Fu Shuang's orphanage in Benxi was magical. It was the one time of the year when the children experienced abundance. In many ways the holiday was like the American Academy Awards, with elegant costumes, delectable food, eccentric celebrations filled with glitz and gold, and awards at the end of the night in the form of presents for the orphans. Red paper lanterns hung everywhere, red couplets – poems and blessings for the coming year – were placed around the doors, and red paper cutouts were pasted on the windows for decorations. Red is a significant color in Chinese culture and represents luck, good fortune, and happiness, as well as being said to ward off evil spirits. It's used heavily during Chinese New Year festivities.

Preparations for the celebration began weeks before the holiday, and the kids were excited from the moment the planning began. In mid-afternoon on the day of the celebration, they were sent to bed so they could wake up just before midnight to celebrate into the early morning hours.

It was every child's favorite holiday because they were given gifts: colorful candy and treats like soda, oranges, peanuts, and sunflower seeds, as well as clothing, pajamas, underwear, and shoes. The children felt special as they carried away new clothing instead of hand-me-downs and were able to fill their bellies instead of going to bed hungry.

In addition to the giving of gifts, the New Year celebration included music. On this special day, the children were allowed to pound on the glossy black Steinway piano in the main hall, draped in garnet silk for the occasion – the only day this lack of discipline was tolerated. Then, sometime during the evening, a hired musician sat down to perform. Orphans, caretakers, and visitors alike embraced the spirit of the evening once the tunes began to play, and everyone sang and danced.

Fireworks and firecrackers came at the end of the night. Fu Shuang and several of the boys at the orphanage stole firecrackers at some point during the night and took them outside – sometimes as far as the park – to set them off. It never occurred to them it was dangerous, and fortunately none of the children were ever injured. Each year they set off their own little stash of firecrackers before returning to watch the rest of the fireworks with the other orphans, delighted at getting away with a little bit of mischief. This behavior would be severely punished any other day of the year, but on this holiday the adults looked the other way. It was the one time of the year the children could rebel a little without fear of repercussions. Chinese New Year was magical and Sierra thought back on it fondly.

—

But she had to admit that preparing for American Christmas was great fun. She enjoyed decorating the house with Christmas garland, lights, ribbons, candy canes, snowmen, Santas, and finding just the right spot for the Holy Family. She loved the festive atmosphere after the tree was trimmed, the stockings hung, and the presents began to appear. She reveled in the Christmas spirit.

Sierra also adored Christmas Eve Mass and dinner with Uncle Brian. It was exciting to get dressed up: she wore a brand-new sheer black skirt and a white long-sleeved shirt with black iridescent trim. She liked the feeling of being part of the larger parish community and she recognized many of the families from weekly mass or from visits to St. John Bosco. She was now part of something spiritual, and although she didn't completely understand the meaning of Christmas, she knew the season was holy and enjoyed the feeling of sacred connection.

Like New Year at the orphanage in Benxi, Christmas in Arizona was enchanting . Sierra couldn't believe her eyes as she looked around the room. There were so many presents! Bright, multicolored lights blinked on the tree, which was topped by a beautiful angel with glistening wings that changed colors. Her stocking was filled to the brim and she found fruity candy, sparkling jewelry, Christmas socks, and a jacks game inside. Santa had brought her a baby doll with all the accessories she could imagine: high chair, crib, clothing, bottles, and diapers. She also found a Barbie doll, clothes, and CDs from Mom and Dad. Mom had put on Christmas music, which played softly as they opened their packages and sipped hot cocoa.

Sierra loved family time. Christmas day with Uncle Bob and Aunt Sheree, Grandma, and her cousins Joe and Kelsee made the day extra special. Christmas brunch was served with ham, potatoes, and a lot of extra side dishes. Most of all, she loved the deviled eggs her "G-ma" made. Everyone ate until their stomachs ached, but a couple of hours later still managed to find room for dessert. Sierra didn't particularly like the pumpkin pie, but she liked the cookies and candy just fine, and savored Uncle Bob's Polish poppy-seed rolls. She couldn't believe how much food there was.

On this first Christmas, 2004, Sierra thought back on her last Chinese New Year celebration, nearly a year earlier. She remembered setting off fireworks with Sheng and Fu Lu, and singing and dancing around the piano with all the other children. Her life had changed dramatically, but she was pleased to know there was an American holiday with festivities and fun, so much like Chinese New Year. Both days seemed to be about celebration, gifts, food, music, and friendship. She embraced Christmas with all her heart.

## Chapter 25:
# Happy Birthday to Me

### Sierra

Sierra's first birthday observance was extremely exciting, and she thought a lot about it ahead of time. It would be the first time anyone had celebrated *her* – ever. She had been to birthday parties since arriving in America, and she knew that they had cake and ice cream, music and games, but other than that they'd all been different, and she had a hard time deciding what kind of a party she wanted to have. Should it be a sleepover with her girlfriends, Chelsea and Justine? That sounded fun, but then her family and other friends wouldn't be there. She could have a dance party and invite all the kids from her class, but then her family would be left out. And, as always, she wanted her family involved.

Finally, she decided.

"I want to have a big birthday bash," she announced. "I want to invite everybody: G-ma, Aunt Sheree and Uncle Bob, Kelsee and Joe and our neighbors and Andree and Brian and Chelsea and Justine and my other friends from school. I want all our family and friends to be there."

"That sounds like a lot of people and a lot of money," said her dad. "Let's have a smaller family party. We can barbeque, have cake and ice cream, play games, and open presents. We're going to be in California for your actual birthday, so this should be on a smaller scale."

"Please?" Sierra begged. "This will be my first birthday celebration. I want to share it with *everyone*."

Her parents looked at each other, then her mom sighed, and with a smile she said, "Let your dad and me talk about it. Whatever we decide, I promise we'll make your birthday great. It's important to us too."

Over the next month, Sierra continued to harp on the need for a large party. Her parents kept trying to steer her toward a smaller celebration, but Sierra persisted. She couldn't tell if she had succeeded in getting her wish, and right up to the day of the party she didn't know what it was going to be like.

On the morning of the festivities, the preparations alone told her she was getting a big party. Her mom bustled around the house, cleaning, putting up decorations, baking, and cooking, helped in each task by Sedona and PJ. Uncle Brian came over early to help as well. The house was festooned with pink and orange streamers, *Lizzy McGuire* decorations, Happy Birthday banners, and multicolored balloons. Her dad prepped the barbeque for burgers, hot dogs, and chicken, and her grandmother brought over Sierra's favorite deviled eggs.

When the guests began to arrive, the music started, and the party began in earnest. Sierra was amazed at the number of guests, the mountain of presents, and the wide array of games and activities her parents had designed for this gala. Everyone Sierra had ever met in America seemed to be at the party, and she was in her element as hostess, happily making introductions.

Her dad dutifully grilled while mom arranged drinks and side dishes in the kitchen. Sedona and PJ greeted friends and ran around the house in a frenzy of excitement. To Sierra it was a joyful sight, and she was delighted with everything.

Soon there were kids and adults swimming in the pool, basking in the sun, and lounging in the hot tub. The pool wasn't built for diving, but that didn't stop the kids from jumping in and splashing everyone sitting nearby. The family's big black Lab, Josie, joined the fun and swam around the pool with the overactive young crowd, her barks of excitement drowned out by the screams of the girls being thrown in the pool by their male classmates. Designated parents watched kids of all ages in the busy aquatic zone, directing the chaos and keeping it under control.

Sierra, like a hummingbird that flits from flower to flower, drifted about the party speaking with everyone. She moved into the room where the quieter kids watched her favorite movie, *Lizzy McGuire*, and commented on her beloved scenes. Then she relocated to the video game room and played Mario Kart with some of the boys. Next, it was on to the food station where she talked to all who would listen about her love for her grandmother's cooking while her G-ma looked on, blushing crimson. Throughout the party, she made sure to talk with kids, relatives, school chums, and family friends, trying hard not to leave anyone out.

The festivities culminated with Sierra opening her presents, followed by ice cream, cake, and the singing of "Happy Birthday." The party had been everything she'd hoped for, and as people began to leave, she thanked each and every one of them for coming to her celebration. Though she usually enjoyed being the center of attention, what she'd loved most was her role as hostess. It felt good to be able to provide food and fun for people she cared about – it was a new sensation to be able to share so much, and she liked it.

When only a few die-hard friends and family members remained, she sat down on the sofa and fell asleep, a radiant smile still on her face.

## Chapter 26:
# Teen Spirit

### Sandi

Sierra turned 13 on May 28, 2005. They didn't celebrate birthdays at the orphanage, and in fact Sierra didn't know her birth date. Though they celebrated birthdays at her boarding school, they did so by the month for all children who had a birthday, so she knew the month but not the day, until we told her. She'd never considered having a personalized birthday blast, but now that she'd been in the United States for a while and had been to other people's birthday parties, she wanted one of her own.

Our house is of average size and can feel a little cramped with just the five of us, so when we were planning Sierra's birthday party, we wanted to keep the crowd manageable. But

Sierra had other ideas. She wanted to invite all her friends from school, extended family, and neighbors, so the guest list was *long*. Add to that the fact that her school friends would be bringing one or both parents, and it got even longer. In the end we had close to seventy people at the party and it was wild. Fun, but wild.

There was food galore. Paul took orders and barbecued throughout the night, without any time to enjoy the party. I never sat down, refreshing snacks and drinks and cleaning up the inevitable messes. Before everyone arrived, PJ and Sedona had helped me decorate the house, and after guests started showing up, the stack of presents in the corner grew and grew. There were kids of all ages creating a bit of chaos in every corner of the house. Outside, older kids jumped, flipped, and squealed with delight on the trampoline, while people of all ages enjoyed the pool. Inside, kids sang karaoke off-key to rock classics like "Don't Stop Believing" and "School's Out." PJ, one of the youngest kids in attendance, was holding court with a bunch of boys aged from toddler to preteen who crowded around the TV playing Nintendo games. Children and adults alike seemed to be having a wonderful time, and none of them more than Sierra herself. She was bouncing around, reveling in her role as master of ceremonies .

One thing she said I'll never forget:

"I can't believe so many people came to celebrate me!"

Her voice was filled with joy, and an innocent delight in the knowledge that nearly a hundred people had come to our house for the express purpose of wishing her well.

But that wasn't the end of our celebration of Sierra's first birthday in America.

—

Every year we go to Orange County, California, to see the Harrises, my sister Barbara's family, and as it turned out, Barbara's and Sierra's birthdays were just a day apart, so this year would be a double celebration.

Barbara and Ron, Barbara's husband, are wonderful people and they made Sierra's first trip to California unforgettable. We barbecued, Barbara made special treats, and there were yet more presents. Barbara's grown daughters, Paula and Lisa, and their families joined in for the party. My eldest brother, Richard, who also lives in California, came to celebrate with us, too. Sierra met her second cousins, Blaze and Hunter, and the kids got to know each other as they played ball, swam, and generally horsed around. Sierra was amazed at all the attention she was getting, and at finding out she had even *more* family. She never stopped smiling.

—

Sierra's actual birthday was spent at Disneyland. She was familiar with Disney characters but didn't know anything about the parks. I'm a huge Disney fan and I couldn't wait to show her the "Happiest Place on Earth." I eagerly watched her face when we walked into the park. Her smile couldn't have been broader as we approached the gate, but once we got inside, she simply looked flabbergasted, her senses overwhelmed by the sights, sounds, and smells around her. I was afraid it might be too much for her, but it wasn't long before excitement took over and she was laughing, skipping, even singing.

I found out that Sierra adored adventure and the fast rides were her favorites. She loved to ride Space Mountain, Thunder Mountain, Tower of Terror, Splash Mountain, and the Matterhorn. The parades and the shows intrigued her, even when she didn't really understand them. She wanted to meet the characters, get their autographs, and take pictures with them. We ate in the California Adventure Park at Ariel's Grotto, which had a Disney character dinner. They celebrated Sierra's birthday with a line dance around the room, and Sierra danced throughout the night with Goofy, then led a line dance with Mickey and Minnie following behind. It was a great way to finish her birthday celebrations.

Around the end of day two, while in line for Space Mountain (again), we turned an unexpected corner. Sierra was listening to her iPod and texting her friends back in Phoenix as we stood with hundreds of other people, waiting our turn.

"I'm bored," she announced suddenly. "It's so boring."

She had become an American teen. I didn't know whether to laugh or cry.

## Chapter 27:
# New School, New Life

### Sierra

Sierra couldn't wait to be at the big public school making new friends. It seemed to her like a graduation of sorts, from childhood to the life of a teenager. But when she came home from school the first day, she was distraught and confused. The teachers had handed her textbooks without explaining anything and told her to read and complete the assignments, even though her English wasn't advanced enough for her to begin to understand her homework. Her parents reassured her and promised to talk with the school about her needs, and told her not worry about the schoolwork. She was encouraged to keep a positive attitude. As this was part of her constitution, she readily accepted the advice.

The next day, Sierra took the bus to school. This was the first time she'd been on a school bus, so she was a little nervous. She slowly walked down the aisle, looking for a place to sit. There were empty seats, but every time Sierra tried to sit down, someone would tell her she couldn't.

"You can't sit there," a dark-haired girl said.

"Why not?" Sierra said innocently.

"Because you're strange and little and annoying."

The bus driver was either oblivious to the situation or simply uninterested, so there was no help from the front of the bus. This happened with an older boy, a petite fair-haired girl, and then another sharp-talking pre-teen wearing leather pants. Finally, another girl insisted that Sierra be allowed to sit in the empty seat next to a quiet boy, but that was the extent of the help offered. This was the first time she'd encountered such "typical" American teen behavior, and Sierra cried softly all the way to school.

The rest of the week was horrific for Sierra. She sobbed every night. She was unable to complete her homework because she just didn't understand it. She told her family stories of kids bullying her and making fun of her. She got up every morning with a smile on her face, determined to win them over, but every afternoon she came home dejected. She would tell her family about her day, and she would dissolve into tears.

"I haven't made any friends," she said through the sobs. "No one will talk to me, sit with me, or eat lunch with me. I'm lonely, frightened, and sad. I thought this school was going to be like DGM and I'd be able to make friends. Why won't they give me a chance?"

# Chapter 28: Time to Learn

## Sandi

Desert Garden Montessori was a great environment for Sierra's introduction to America, but as the end of the school year approached, we realized she was behind academically. By now she spoke and understood English well, but she still needed improvement in reading and writing English, math, and other critical subjects. Paul and I talked to her about leaving DGM and going to a public school that had "English as a Second Language" (ESL) classes for the 2005–06 school year.

This was a big step for Sierra. It meant leaving behind her new friends and classmates, starting over again, meeting new people, and finding her place in a new environment. She was sad as she finished the school year, but her natural optimism made her hopeful about the future.

We decided on Akimel A-al Middle School, the public school in our district. They had an ESL program and the appropriate educational resources to address her particular needs and get her up to speed where she'd fallen behind during the previous year. The school would also require her to interact with more children her own age. Sierra was excited to be attending a "big school," and as the new school year approached, her enthusiasm increased. She'd had such a great experience at DGM that she expected her experiences at the public school to be just as positive.

Akimel A-al Middle School is two miles, about ten minutes, from our home, so it was certainly convenient. The school is part of the Kyrene School District, which had a great reputation in the Phoenix area. The name of the school is taken from the Akimel O'odham Reservation nearby and means "People of the River." The school had over a thousand students across grades six through eight, with a teacher-student ratio of twenty to one, which was about the same as DGM. But it had certified ESL teachers, which was critical to advancing Sierra's academic career.

Before we enrolled her as a seventh grader, we talked to the administrators about her unusual situation. They seemed to have a good grasp of the challenges she faced because of her background and recent major life upheavals, which was encouraging. We emphasized the need for her to begin to study other subjects as well as improve her English skills, and they expressed agreement. We all seemed to be on the same page.

As it happened, we weren't on the same page at all. We weren't even reading the same book. After the first days of school, it became apparent that Sierra was not getting ESL classes, was being bullied, and was miserable. It broke our hearts to see our friendly, generous, kind daughter so distressed. So I started making calls.

I called the school administrators, trying to find out if Sierra had been assigned an ESL class or if she had a liaison who could assist her during the school day when she was confused. I spent a lot of time on the phone being transferred from person to person and simply couldn't get any satisfactory answers to my questions. Eventually I made an appointment to see the principal and several of Sierra's teachers that Friday. I called Paul and we decided we should both go, since we wanted them to know how concerned we were about our daughter's dilemma and make them understand we needed their assistance.

The meeting on Friday turned out to be with twenty of the school's staff, including the principal. Paul and I opened by talking about Sierra's learning challenges and how we hoped Akimel could help her succeed. I suggested it would be helpful for her to have an interpreter or at least a student she could be paired with to assist her. After about fifteen minutes of us talking and them staring at us vacantly, I asked if they could please respond, and let us know what ideas they had for helping our daughter.

The principal, looking at us without sympathy or understanding, informed us that they couldn't and wouldn't be doing anything different or special for Sierra. They explained that the Kyrene School District would only put a child in an ESL classroom if English was not the primary language spoken at home. We spoke English at home, therefore Sierra was not entitled to be in an ESL class.

I was stunned. "You mean you never had any intention helping her with English? She spoke Mandarin Chinese her entire life, and only began speaking English less than a year ago. She doesn't understand anything being said in her classes, and she can't do her homework or assignments."

"I'm sorry, but we can't make special accommodations for your daughter," the principal said coldly. "The district rules just don't allow us to make exceptions. Sierra will have to learn in the same environment and follow the same rules as everyone else."

No one else in the room had anything to add, and not one person so much as expressed genuine regret that they were unable to help. I reminded the principal of our previous conversation over the summer regarding Sierra's special requirements, and she didn't respond. I asked again, and waited.

"Do you remember our conversation?" I said.

"I didn't know that the only language spoken at home was English," she said.

"How could you not have known? If you didn't know and it was required, you should have asked," I said firmly.

No response was forthcoming. The meeting appeared to be over.

"So much for no child left behind. It's inspiring to meet such caring educators," I said, furious, as Paul and I left.

I couldn't believe it. This was supposed to be a great school in an excellent school district, yet they clearly had zero concern for the success of our daughter. Now it was my turn for the waterworks. Tears of frustration rolled down my face as we drove home.

"What are we going to do, Paul?"

"I don't know. What can we do?"

I thought for a moment as I sniffled, then an idea struck me. "I'm going to speak with an attorney at work and get some legal advice. Surely an ESL school *has* to provide English to the students without English proficiency."

Unfortunately, my lawyer friend at work told me we'd probably need to employ an attorney who could research the situation and threaten litigation. If we wanted to get the Kyrene School District to change their position, it might be necessary to sue them. This was discouraging. I didn't know where we would get the funds for this endeavor, and in the meantime, Sierra would fall further behind in her schoolwork and would continue to be frustrated and miserable at school. I also realized that Paul and I had planned to address the bullying issue in our meeting at Akimel, but we hadn't gotten that far. After seeing how they dealt with academics, I didn't have much faith in their desire to help Sierra with social problems.

Over the weekend, I came up with another solution: we could pull her out of Akimel and move her to St. John Bosco, the Catholic school that Sedona and PJ attended. A private Catholic school might not be equipped to handle an ESL student, but at least we knew they would be kind, compassionate, and accepting. It seemed to me that this acceptance would be a critical component of any learning environment in which Sierra could excel.

The only issue would be convincing SJB to take her.

St. John Bosco was doing a great job with Sedona and PJ. It had opened several years earlier and quickly developed a reputation for academic excellence in a faith-based curriculum. In fact, there was a waiting list for kindergarten and several of the lower grades. Mr. Elliot, the principal, was a no-nonsense administrator who did not accept bullying or intolerance at the school. He was admired by parents, students, teachers, and staff, and I had the greatest respect for him. I knew that even if he wasn't persuaded to accept Sierra as a student, he would provide excellent counsel on how to go about finding a school that would be a good fit for her.

I made an appointment and prepared my speech for Mr. Elliot. I didn't want to be melodramatic, but we were panic-stricken at this point, praying for a solution that would allow Sierra to flourish. We were worried about both her education and her happiness, so I wasn't beyond pleading and making promises to do anything he asked if he'd just agree to take her in.

When I got up the morning of my meeting with Mr. Elliot, I was so filled with apprehension my chest felt tight. It was a hot summer day with the weather in the 100s, but I went outside to breathe in the searing desert air and center myself before I left for the school. I sat in a cobalt-blue folding chair in the front of our house and took deep breaths. A saguaro cactus in our yard cradled a dove's nest in one arm, and I watched as the mother dove cooed and fed her chicks.

"Do you worry about your babies too?" I asked her, feeling a kinship with this little creature. Her babies might not face the same problems as mine, but I was sure she felt the same need to protect hers that I did.

I met Mr. Elliot at about 9:30. He was an intelligent and kind man with a thoughtful face, dressed in business attire that looked slightly formal for the elementary school environment. He knew our family already, so he greeted me with a big smile and a strong handshake.

"Mrs. Wilson," he said. "So nice to see you." Not one for small talk, he immediately asked, "What's the subject today?" since I hadn't told him the reason for my visit.

My heart pounded as I recounted Sierra's story, including the academic challenges, the bullying, the lack of administrative support, and our desire to have Sierra in a loving, Christ-based environment. He listened intently, frowning. I wondered if it was because as an educator he was upset, or if it was because he didn't feel he had a solution for her at SJB, and my heart began to accelerate.

"Mrs. Wilson," he said when I had finished, "I am so sorry you're going through this. It's certainly unfair, but SJB just doesn't have the capacity to take Sierra in. I don't have any ESL-certified teachers or special programs. I hate to say it, but I don't think our school is the best solution for her."

This wasn't what I wanted to hear, but at least when he said he was sorry he actually looked and sounded like he meant it.

I had halfway been expecting this response, but I was ready with counterarguments.

"We don't really have any other options. The Montessori school was great for her at first, but they're not prepared to bring her to the next level. They don't have an ESL program either and their resources are more limited than yours. They weren't teaching her math, science, social studies, or even English reading and comprehension. It was a good solution to get her to learn conversational English, but they can't continue to educate her. I believe God brought her to our family for a reason and I believe this school is our academic solution. I have the greatest faith in your school's ability to help her. I'm open to any ideas you may have."

Mr. Elliot sat with his head in his hands, thinking silently, for about five minutes. And as he thought, I prayed.

Slowly, a smile spread over his face, and I felt the first glimmer of hope.

"Would you be willing to have Sierra receive tutoring after school? It would be an additional cost, not included in your tuition."

I nodded enthusiastically. "Yes! We'd be glad to supplement her education with tutoring."

"What if we begin Sierra in first grade reading? She'd work her way up the grade levels, and we'll get her as far as we can in the next two years. We'll assess her math skills and do the same thing with that subject. We'll put her in a seventh grade homeroom class so she can make friends with kids her own age, and we'll have her go to religion, science, social studies, music, and PE whenever we can. It will be unconventional, but it just might work."

It was my turn to smile. I told him it sounded perfect and thanked him profusely for being willing to treat Sierra like an individual, with care and a desire to help her get the education she needed and deserved. As I left, I was in tears again, but this time it was tears of joy.

I immediately called Paul and he and I rejoiced that we had found a solution, giving thanks for Mr. Elliot. We both had great faith in the school's ability to provide our daughter with a first-rate education. God and Saint John Bosco himself were looking after Sierra.

## Chapter 29:
# St. John Bosco Saves the Day

### Sierra

Sierra left Akimel for St. John Bosco in August 2005, and her experience at SJB was different from day one. Before her arrival, her classmates were fully briefed on Sierra's background and the challenges she faced. They were told how lucky they were to have her at their school and what a unique opportunity had been given to them to help her acclimate to American life and learn about another culture. They were told to make her feel welcome and accepted, and they did so in spades.

The first person Sierra met at SJB was Ms. Patrice Whalen, an earthy person who dressed in khaki shorts with either

T-shirts or casual collared shirts. She was the junior high science teacher and Sierra's homeroom instructor. Ms. Whalen was passionate about science, even obsessed with it, but in Sierra's case, science wasn't going to be her top priority. Instead, she made sure that her students were respectful and helpful. Mrs. Whalen acted as Sierra's protector, cheerleader, encouragement coach, and advocate as well as educator. She made it her goal to ensure Sierra was provided with the assistance and support she so desperately needed, especially after her disastrous experience at Akimel.

Patrice Whalen was also a bit ... eccentric. When Sierra first walked into her new homeroom, her eyes nearly popped out. There were birds, rodents, reptiles, and fish, and Sierra didn't like it at all. She had come to accept Josie and Barkley, but she still wasn't comfortable around animals, and now every day she was confronted with the sights, sounds, and smells of this menagerie. The squeaking and shrieking of the timid guinea pigs as they scurried around their cages made her nervous. She loathed the lime green snake that slept coiled up in the corner of a large glass aquarium. The iguana on its tawny brown stick scared her, with its eyes looking in different directions as if to say *I can see you no matter where you are.* The little yellow-and-black finches that chirped happily, singing to the beauty of the day, bothered her less, as did the vibrant topical fish that swam around their tank in endless circles. Animals simply weren't her thing, yet because of her respect for her homeroom teacher, Sierra slowly began to feel a guarded respect for the classroom's furred, feathered, scaled, and finned denizens, too.

Ms. Whalen wasn't the only staff member giving Sierra extra attention and support; all the teachers and administrators provided words of praise and showed willingness to spend additional time with her. But two teachers went above and beyond: Mrs. Perkins, Sierra's first-grade English teacher, and Mrs. Hernandez, her fifth-grade math teacher.

There was an age difference of anywhere from three to seven years between Sierra and the other students in these classes, but it was vital for Sierra to be able to progress with other students at her own level in both subjects. Mrs. Perkins and Mrs. Hernandez had told the other students in their classes that they were part of a grand experiment, and that having Sierra in their rooms was a privilege, so rather than anyone feeling uncomfortable or awkward, they all felt part of something special. As always, Sierra was notably good with the small children, and would give the first graders high fives, help them with small tasks, and generally be a positive force in the classroom.

One day during circle time in Mrs. Perkin's class, the children talked about striking a match. To Sierra, the word "match" meant pairing up similar objects. But this time, the subject was lighting a match and creating an unintentional fire. This confused Sierra.

*Why would matching words or objects create a fire?*

Seeing the puzzled look on Sierra's face, Mrs. Perkins asked her what was wrong. Sierra voiced her bewilderment and the class laughed. Mrs. Perkins explained to her that English is difficult to learn as a second language because so many words have multiple meanings. The kids quickly apologized to Sierra, and she joined in the laughter about her confusion. She left class that day understanding that learning English would continue to be a struggle, but confident that she would get there in the end.

Sierra was learning, growing and loving her school. She was part of the SJB community, and they accepted and embraced her. As a bonus, Sedona was there with her, attending third grade, and the girls often spotted each other throughout the day. Sedona, shy and reserved, would see Sierra laughing and talking and being her outgoing self, and was baffled at her confidence. Sierra wanted to be noticed and acknowledged, while Sedona wanted to fade into the background. Despite their differences, the girls got along well and were happy to be at the same school.

PJ was in Pre-Kindergarten, and his classroom wasn't on the main campus with his sisters, but on a remote campus at our parish church. In the morning I dropped his sisters off at SJB, then took him to Corpus Christi Catholic Church. He missed being with his biggest sister, and Sierra missed being with him as well, but all three of them got to be together at SJB events, which were always held on the main campus.

At the end of Sierra's first year at SJB, the seventh graders put on a play and were asked to take the part of their patron saint. Earlier that year, Sierra had chosen Joan of Arc during the Sacrament of Confirmation, because she felt St. Joan epitomized the courage she tried to show in her own life. Like Joan, Sierra's life had changed dramatically when she was an adolescent, and like Joan, Sierra believed in following her heart. To Sierra, St. Joan represented her own goal of being "more than just a girl." She didn't think it was fair that the boys traditionally had adventurous and daring jobs. Like St. Joan, Sierra didn't want to be boxed into the girl's role. She wanted to be exceptional, no matter her gender.

But Sierra was still struggling with English, and now she was expected to write and deliver a speech in front of the entire student body *and* parents. She was terrified, but using St. Joan as her model, she put her faith in God and refused to give in to fear. She worked hard at the assignment, practiced her speech until she had it memorized perfectly, and in the end, she was proud of what she presented.

"It was the most difficult assignment all year, but I'm glad I did it," she said later.

—

Sierra continued to be successful at SJB and stayed there until she graduated to high school. She was the shortest kid in her class, but it didn't stop her from playing sports. She was active and outgoing, running for class president and singing in the choir, and because she regularly moved between elementary and junior high classes, she made friends in almost every grade. She knew families as well as students and was liked by all of them. She began to get babysitting jobs, as the younger children loved her energy and positive attitude and the parents trusted her to be responsible.

When it came time to graduate in 2007, Sierra was heartbroken to leave her beloved school. Her parents would have loved for her to continue in parochial school, but unfortunately, the Catholic high schools wouldn't enroll her because of her results on the entrance exams. She was making great progress with English and math, but she was still behind, so Sierra would be attending a public school in the fall: Desert Vista High School.

The eighth-grade promotion and associated activities were great fun for Sierra and her fellow students. Bittersweet parties, celebrations, and ceremonies took place during the whole last month of school, well attended by students and their families. There were private graduation parties as well. Of course, Sierra wanted to attend every affair and festivity she could. Most of Sierra's friends were going to Catholic high schools, so she would again have to find new friends and blaze her own path in high school.

The graduation Mass at SJB was a solemn event. The graduates sat in the first pews at St. Benedict's, dressed in their best outfits. Sierra wore a formal soft pink chiffon dress and looked almost like a miniature doll next to the other students. She was four feet, six inches and, according to her pediatrician, had finished growing. Most of her classmates had experienced huge growth spurts. With the other girls and boys towering above her, Sierra was like a tiny ficus tree planted among redwoods. But her little tree was shining with Christmas lights as she glowed with pride in her place on the pew.

The graduation ceremony was held at the end of the Mass, and teachers and administrators related achievements and stories about the class of 2007, then spoke about each child. When Mrs. Duvall, the eighth-grade English teacher, spoke about Sierra her voice cracked and she began to cry.

"Sierra has become an inspiration to the entire school," she said. "The progress she's made during her journey at St. John Bosco has been miraculous. Sierra has given back to the school with her optimism and drive to learn."

Sierra was deeply touched, and as she looked around the room, she saw many people affected by Ms. Duval's speech. Sierra's mom's face was soaked with tears, and her sleeve was drenched by the time the family left the church.

Sierra beamed through it all. She seemed filled with confidence. She walked with a skip in her step and a mammoth smile on her face, talking and laughing with her classmates as they discussed the years ahead and gave promises to stay in touch.

Throughout that summer after graduation, Sierra watched the video the school had prepared for the graduating class and knew she would truly miss SJB. St. John Bosco had been a place of acceptance, belonging, and peace. Now she faced yet another new beginning.

After what happened with Akimel, Sierra was understandably concerned about going back to public school, but her parents assured her Desert Vista wouldn't be like Akimel. Sierra hoped they were right.

## Chapter 30:
# The High School Experience Begins

Sandi

Desert Vista High School (DVHS) was established in 1996 and was only two and a half miles from our house. The school was huge, with over three thousand students and graduating classes of more than eight hundred. DVHS was classified as an "excelling" school and had won the "A+ School of Excellence Award." Because the school was known for its high standardized test scores and academic excellence, we thought it was a great choice for Sierra's next step. Despite the enormous size of the student body, it had the credentials to provide her with the education she needed to graduate on time and with English and math proficiency.

However, we were nervous about Sierra attending another public school, based on the experience that she had in middle school. Before she was enrolled, Paul and I went to Desert Vista to speak with the principal and vice principal. We were assured that Sierra would be in ESL classes and would be put on an individualized education program (IEP). The administrators further promised that she would graduate proficient in English and math, and that they would make sure she passed the AIMS test (Arizona's Instrument to Measure Standards), the standardized assessment required at that time by the State of Arizona for a student to graduate. We were hopeful DVHS would be a good fit and provide the support Sierra needed.

—

Although the Phoenix area has a diverse population, Ahwatukee has a reputation for being predominantly white – it's sometimes referred to as "All-White-Tukee." This was reflected in the makeup of the student body at DVHS as well the fact that 62 percent of the student population was white. Fewer than 10 percent of the three thousand students were categorized as Asian. At this point, we didn't know what that might mean for Sierra. She was used to being different, but she was also used to being considered an asset and a special member of her school. Here at Desert Vista she might be just another face among many, most of those faces looking more like her adoptive parents than herself.

DVHS's campus was as large as many community colleges, and I was very concerned about the impersonal aspects of such a big school. (The entire student body of SJB during Sierra's last year was 525 students.) Making the adjustment to Desert Vista was not going to be easy, and I knew Sierra was worried, which concerned me even more.

Sierra obtained wisdom at SJB that was not purely academic. She learned about social justice, confidence, and self-acceptance. These new virtues would serve her well at DV.

## Chapter 31:
# Launching the High School Experience

### Sierra

Sierra's first day at Desert Vista was unlike anything she had experienced before. Her mom dropped her off at the gate and she made her way into the school with the rest of the teens. They looked like a herd of cows squeezing through a small gate, in no hurry to get onto the campus. Sierra was swallowed up in the crowd, and being so much shorter than everyone else, it was impossible for her to see over the others as she walked. Still, she had a positive outlook, a smile on her face, and a determination to make it an amazing year. She quickly realized how different this environment was from SJB. The girls dressed in grubby jeans and T-shirts or short, tight skirts with high heels and low-cut tops, and everything in between. The boys mostly wore jeans and T-shirts with athletic shoes. However, some of the T-shirts had messages that would not have been allowed at her elementary school. This was a whole different world.

She was a little frightened as she walked through the campus that first day, trying desperately to find her classes before the bell rang. The school was four times the size of St. John Bosco, and it was two stories. There were many buildings and she had only five minutes to change classrooms, which were spread out in all corners of the campus. This added to her stress and tension. Sierra had a full schedule and she was anxious to get started, but the butterflies in her stomach made it difficult to relax into the day. She struggled to understand the instructions of her teachers, but she did notice that the teachers were patient and attentive. This was a good sign.

Her fellow students were not welcoming. The kids appeared to have established friendships, and all knew each other. They either ignored her, sneered at her, or were generally rude. Even on the very first day, some boys make crude comments to her. She was determined not be bullied like she was at Akimel and vowed to herself to tell someone if the behavior persisted.

*I don't deserve this, I don't need it, and I won't put up with it.*

By the end of the first week, kids were still making fun of her size, following her around, and verbally abusing her. On the way to her math class one of the vulgar boys snatched at her behind as she went up the stairs. He grabbed and held on tightly, following her up the staircase. Sierra was furious and scared. She couldn't believe someone deemed it acceptable to violate her body. She felt it was an attempt to intimidate her and make her submissive, which was intolerable. That night, she told her parents. Her mom said she would call the principal on Monday, but also told Sierra to make an appointment with her counselor to discuss the issue directly.

The administration reacted quickly and had security personnel walking Sierra to her classrooms the very next day. Sierra pointed out the perpetrators as she went to her classes, even though she was nervous about doing this.

"What if the school doesn't take care of it?" she asked her parents. "What if the boys become even more abusive?" Her parents assured her that they would deal with any fallout that occurred, but to proceed with confidence that the school would be good to their word.

The boys who tormented her were brought into the vice principal's office and told to stop immediately or face the consequences, which could include suspension. They chose to stop. Sierra's faith in the school skyrocketed.

# Chapter 32: High School Drama

## Sandi

Though some of the students were not kind to Sierra, the teachers were exceptionally helpful. As promised, she was enrolled in ESL classes and provided with an IEP that addressed her specific needs. Paul and I grew increasingly confident that the administrators and staff genuinely cared about her success and paid attention to her progress. Sierra liked her classes and her new teachers. All the adults at the school, from the librarian to the janitor, loved Sierra, and the administration let me know that she was a treasure. It was good to realize she was appreciated and valued. We felt certain that with her sunny disposition and outgoing nature, it was only a matter of time before she made new friends.

—

After the bullying at DVHS stopped, Sierra had to endure bullying once again from students at another school, though it was some time before we found out about it. Sedona and PJ were attending St. John Bosco, and Sierra enjoyed spending time there after school. Sierra rode the school bus to the final stop, which was close to SJB. Then, Paul picked all the kids up on his way home from work. On her walk to St. John Bosco, Sierra had to pass Horizon Honor School, a charter school that had students grades K–12. When she'd get off the bus, Horizon kids were getting out of school, and several of their high school kids began to harass her daily. They called her names, yelled out obscenities, gave her the finger, and even threw stones at her. This bullying became increasingly worse as time progressed.

Sierra went to great lengths to avoid the Horizon kids by walking on the other side of the street and not crossing at the crosswalk by Horizon. Instead, she walked to the next traffic light, which was considerably farther. Even on the other side of the street she avoided looking at them, but the one time she glanced their way, they were staring at her. Having her attention, they all flipped her off and began laughing. Her tolerance gave out.

When she came home from school, she finally told us what had been happening. She wasn't as tearful as she'd been during her trials at middle school, but she was shaken and upset, and confessed she dreaded her walk from the bus stop to SJB every day.

"All I want is to be left alone to find my own place. I feel like this is never going to occur. Flipping me off might not have been that big a deal but combined with everything else, it is just too much."

I was beginning to feel that most high school students were mean and angry. I knew this wasn't the case, but tiny Sierra was an anomaly some kids just couldn't leave alone. I called Horizon and explained the situation. It was strange to tell *their* administrators that *my* teen, who didn't even attend Horizon, was being bullied by *their* students. They were appalled. I'm happy to say that Horizon's school administrators immediately put a stop to the harassment.

Bullies exist in all phases of life, sadly, and Sierra had learned an important lesson. Rather than running away or hiding from a bad situation, she learned to face it head-on, stand tall, and not let other people make her feel bad about herself. Now, looking back, she and I agree these experiences were integral to who Sierra has become. They have allowed her to be an advocate for those who have endured similar situations, as she can empathize and share what worked for her.

—

For most students in Arizona, the AIMS test was a necessary evil, a hurdle to overcome the way to graduation. For Sierra, it was a significant sign of achievement. We knew that if she passed the AIMS test, she would not only graduate, but she'd be armed with the basic educational skills she'd need for whatever she chose to do in life.

Children who attend public schools begin taking AIMS preparation tests in the sixth grade, but because Sierra went to SJB and the AIMS tests aren't required for private schools, she hadn't taken any preparatory tests. The real test would be administered in the students' sophomore year, but DVHS began practice testing students in their freshman year. Many students passed during their first examination, in which case they were through with the test. But students who didn't pass continued to be retested all through senior year, until they passed or ultimately failed and didn't graduate.

Sierra's first attempt was the freshman-year practice test, and it showed how far behind she was academically. But Sierra, being Sierra, wasn't discouraged. DVHS had extensive remedial English classes after school for students who needed additional reading comprehension assistance, and she began attending them regularly, working hard to increase her reading and writing skills. Her English grades improved, but she still didn't pass the standardized test in her sophomore year. The test was administered twice in Sierra's junior year: fall and spring. In the fall, she took the test for the third time and failed again.

At this point, the test had become a source of anxiety for her. It was a stigma at school if you were still taking the test past your sophomore year, and she began to worry about what would happen if she couldn't pass. She became obsessed and talked about the test constantly. All I could do was reassure her that I had faith in her ability, and I knew that she would pass, despite my own concerns. I didn't tell her, but I even talked to her counselor at DV about what would happen if she never did pass, just so I'd be prepared.

Sierra's teachers and counselors were all on her side, cheering her on and sending her positive messages. Then, one of her counselors, Mrs. Jones, watched Sierra while she was testing and noticed that Sierra mouthed the words she was reading. Mrs. Jones decided that Sierra should be put in a room by herself, so she could read out loud while the test was being administered. Mrs. Jones surmised that reading aloud would help Sierra comprehend the questions and better answer them. This was an out-of-the-ordinary request and needed to be approved by personnel at the highest level, which took some time, but eventually, the plan was given the green light.

So, during the spring of her junior year, Sierra sat alone in a room with a test administrator and read the test questions aloud. This was the magic ticket Sierra needed. The summer before her senior year we learned that she had passed.

We were enormously relieved and grateful, but not nearly as relieved and grateful as she was that it was all over and she'd succeeded. Her diligence and determination had resulted in this major accomplishment, and she was proud of herself. One of the best outcomes of the whole agonizing process was Sierra's increased self-confidence. This achievement was a sign of academic success that she had rarely experienced since coming to America. Not only had she learned a valuable lesson in persistence and hard work, but she was free to enjoy her senior year at Desert Vista.

## Chapter 33:
# The Teen Years

### Sierra

Her schoolwork was difficult but rewarding. She realized she was making progress and learning at a faster pace than ever before. Her teachers were excellent, and she was working hard. She also pushed herself to make friends. She talked with kids in her classes and sat with other girls on benches around campus during breaks. Sierra had never been shy, and her ability to strike up a conversation with a total stranger was exactly what was needed in her new situation. She gradually began to create her own social circle.

Sierra did have one friend whom she knew prior to attending Desert Vista – Kathy. They had met when Sierra was at SJB, even though Kathy was homeschooled. Sierra's mom and Kathy's dad both served on the SJB Advisory Board, and because their daughters had similar backgrounds – Kathy was adopted from Peru as a baby –they were introduced. Like Sierra, Kathy was short, outgoing, happy, and funny. The two girls hit it off immediately. They saw each other regularly when Sierra was in seventh and eighth grade and were delighted to be going to the same high school. While they didn't have classes together, they did carpool to and from school each day.

Soon after school began, Kathy was selected for the freshman cheer squad and quickly acquired a boyfriend. Sierra didn't run in the same crowd and had no interest in having a boyfriend. Kathy talked about boys all the time and was boy crazy. Sierra didn't want or need a boyfriend and grew tired of Kathy's obsession. They didn't have similar school interests either; Sierra concentrated on her academics, while Kathy was more interested in the social aspects of school. They were growing away from each other but still considered themselves friends.

One afternoon in the spring of her freshman year, Sierra was called into the vice principal's office. There had been some trouble with Kathy, her boyfriend, and her other friends. The school knew that Sierra and Kathy were pals, so Sierra was called in as a witness. As it turned out, Sierra wasn't involved with the situation and was removed from the witness list. However, this left Sierra feeling vulnerable and unhappy, like she'd done something wrong. It was the first time she'd ever been called into administration for a disciplinary issue, in America or China, and she didn't like it. Even though she wasn't in trouble, she took it as a warning sign and stopped hanging out and carpooling with Kathy, though the girls remained cordial. Sierra was saddened to lose a friend, but she was determined to do what was right for her. She was growing up and learning about responsibility.

During her high school years, Sierra noticed she was most happy when she was helping others, so she decided to spread the love. She began to send daily texts and social media posts with positive messages to family and friends – things like "Have a great day!" and "Believe in yourself!" Her encouragement was noticed and appreciated by everyone who received it, and she felt blessed. This was another indication of Sierra's growing maturity. She was becoming passionate about people and spreading kindness.

—

During the summer after her sophomore year, the family took a trip to Disney's Hilton Head Island Resort. Instead of going straight there, her parents decided to go to Florida and drive up the coast, through Georgia, and on into South Carolina. The coastal area of Florida was arrayed with palm trees, silvery-white beaches, and beautiful orange and gold Gaillardia, also called the blanket flower, along the sandy shorelines. When the Wilsons drove into Georgia, they moved inland and saw tree-lined streets with live oaks trailing Spanish moss like tattered old sheets. It was a little spooky but beautiful. Sedona and PJ were amazed at the lush scenery – it was greener than any topography they'd seen before – and Sierra loved the old Southern buildings.

One of the family's rest stops was in Fort Valley, Georgia, at a Chick-fil-A. It was the Wilsons' first time interacting with the residents in Georgia. Strangely, the patrons in the restaurant appeared to be staring at Sierra, her siblings, and her parents. This certainly wasn't the first time such a thing had happened, but it appeared to be more blatant than normal.

"I guess they haven't ever seen a family with two white parents, two Asian girls, and a Hispanic boy," Sierra said. "Don't they know about adoption?"

The Wilsons were laughing about her comment when a group of men and women dressed in eighteenth-century clothes arrived in a horse and carriage, and another group stepped out of a black car. The women wore long, sky-blue prairie dresses with white lace trim and white bonnets on their heads; the men were dressed in old-fashioned black suits, with white collarless buttoned shirts. As the family later discovered after an Internet search, these were Georgia Beachy Amish Mennonites. They came into the restaurant as Sierra and her family sat down to eat. The kids stared at them, and they stared back. Their mom reminded them that staring was rude, but both groups continued to look at each other intently.

Sierra took the approach she always did when people stared at her family, and gave the other folks a friendly, "Hello, how's it going?" Sierra had been coached to say this by Cari, one of her mom's friends at work. Cari was the spokesperson for Maricopa County government, so she was on TV a lot, and she was highly respected in the Phoenix community. Cari had told Sierra to be bold, unapologetic, and outgoing. Cari was all of those things, and since Sierra looked up to her, she always tried to follow advice Cari gave her.

The Mennonites didn't respond to Sierra's greeting but continued to stare. After the Wilson clan returned to their car, they agreed that perhaps both groups were unusual, and that was okay.

"We need to remember that when other people stare at us," Sierra's mom said. "It doesn't mean they're being judgmental. They're just curious. It's human."

—

Once in Hilton Head, the family embarked on a dolphin tour. A young guide took the family out from the Disney Resort on a small power boat to see dolphins in the wild. It was a sunny day, the cool blue ocean water was calm, and there were a lot of dolphin mothers and babies swimming in the shallow water near the resort.

Everyone loved seeing the dolphins swim with their calves, and the tour guide was both knowledgeable and entertaining. As the guide steered the boat around the bay, he told the Wilsons the names he'd given all the dolphins he regularly saw, and explained their personalities – some were shy, others talkative, and others energetic. Just as the group was leaving to go into deeper waters to see dolphins jumping and playing, the guide suddenly stopped the boat. One of the dolphins, Popper, made a beeline for them. He jumped up onto the side of the boat and stared at Sierra. "Hello there," Sierra said to the dolphin. Popper looked around at each member of the family, then, just as quickly as he'd appeared, flipped back out into the ocean.

The guide was amazed at this behavior and said it had only happened to him once before, even though he was out on the water every day during the summer.

"Dolphins are highly intelligent and curious," he said. "The last time this happened I was in the boat with a man using an oxygen tank. The dolphin heard it and wanted a better look. Popper must have been interested in something in this boat."

He looked around for clues. Then he said, "I think he was looking at Sierra. I think he saw the glitter of your bling, Sierra, and wanted a closer look."

Everyone laughed. PJ and Sedona often teased Sierra about her fondness for bling and being the center of attention, but on this day, her bling brought us all a dolphin named Popper.

—

When Sierra turned sixteen, she got a call from the principal at St. John Bosco, Shelley Conner. Mrs. Conner wanted to hire a teen to help with the after-school program and she asked Sierra if she was available and willing to come in for an interview. Sierra was thrilled, and after her interview she was offered the job. It was her first job other than babysitting, and she loved it. The duties including helping the kids with homework and keeping an eye on them. She'd walk to SJB from her bus stop, stay until SJB closed, then ride her bike home. It was perfect.

Working at St. John Bosco helped Sierra become more confident and self-reliant. She developed friendships with school administrators and teachers, and got to know many of the families of the children who attended the school, which led to more babysitting jobs. Sierra helped in the classrooms, encouraged and guided the kids in athletics, and danced with them to pop music. She was a fun but firm authority figure, and she thrived on the responsibility. Every day she wrote a phase of encouragement on the white board like, "You are enough," "Be kind to each other," and "Love life." Sierra was a role model for the students, and they came to her with their problems. If they were being bullied, she was the one they confided in. If they were having self-confidence crises, they would seek out her advice. If they needed coaching in just about anything, Sierra was the "go-to" caretaker.

She also chaperoned the school dances and was the master of ceremonies at many school events, even acting as DJ on occasion. In the time since coming to America, she'd learned to enjoy all kinds of music, but her favorite genre was still pop. Eventually, her school experience and love of music led to a side job as a DJ for a local firm owned by a parent.

In addition to all these after-school activities, Sierra was still working hard at school, and this busy schedule put a strain on her social activities. Unlike many of her girlfriends, Sierra wasn't dating. This meant that when she went to football games, dances, and other high school events, the dynamics changed. Couples branched off and Sierra was often left with smaller groups of kids she didn't know as well, who were also not into the dating scene. Sierra was comfortable not dating, but she did notice that it made her stand out in a new way.

Sierra made many friends throughout her years in high school, and in fact was so popular she was nominated for homecoming queen during her senior year. This was quite an accomplishment for a girl who'd come to America only seven years earlier. When she found out about the homecoming queen nomination, she dove into preparations, which included finding the right dress and getting her hair fixed. So she scheduled a visit with Heidi, her hair stylist.

"Please make me look fabulous," Sierra told Heidi as she worked on her hair the day of the event.

"Of course," Heidi said. "Who's your date for homecoming? Is he handsome?"

Sierra turned beet red and shook her head. "I don't have a date. I don't need a date. I'm going with a group," she said.

"Do the other girls in homecoming court have dates?" Heidi asked.

"I think so, but I'm not defined by a man. I don't want a date, Heidi," Sierra said firmly.

And not having a date didn't impact her enjoyment of the big day in the least. She was radiant and affable as she rode the float during halftime. She was euphoric, her confidence riding high on this unforgettable night.

She graduated from DVHS in May 2011, and this milestone was something she was very proud of. She had passed the AIMS test, received good grades in her classes, worked hard, and it had paid off. Life was good, and she was on her way.

# Chapter 34: Maricopa County and Buddha

Sandi

In 2008, my work life became a nightmare. I was the deputy county manager and budget director for Maricopa County, and had been for over twenty years. Most of my time there had been productive and fulfilling, and I enjoyed it. However, there was a two-year time period that was simply hellish, and it had an impact on not just my work life but also my family life.

In November , Don Stapley, a member of the Maricopa Board of Supervisors, was indicted on 118 felony counts related to improperly completed campaign paperwork -- charges that were ultimately dismissed.The County Board of Supervisors was in distress because of the situation with Supervisor Stapley and the recessionary financial cycle. Stapley's prosecution marked the beginning of a political war that spanned several years and left chaos in its wake. In addition to Mr. Stapley, board member Mary Rose Wilcox was also indicted, on a charge that was also later dismissed.

Maricopa County is not only the largest county in Arizona, but the fourth-largest county in the country with four million residents. The county government employed about twelve thousand of those residents at the time. There were approximately thirty-five departments overseen by the Board of Supervisors, under the direction of the County Manager, while an additional seven independently elected officers oversaw the rest of the county departments. This meant that they reported directly to the electorate. The judicial branch was also an independent branch of state government, funded by Maricopa County taxpayers.

As the Deputy County Manager, I oversaw many departments, including Correctional Health, Public Health, Information Technology, Human Resources, Risk Management, and the Office of Management and Budget. I was responsible for developing a budget of over $2 billion.

The year 2008 was the beginning of the Great Recession, which hit Arizona particularly hard since construction and housing played a large role in the state's economy. In Maricopa County, the bottom fell out of the housing market, job growth stopped, and the economy – which had been growing – came to an abrupt halt. The Board of Supervisors decided not to raise taxes for the budget shortfall, believing it would worsen the economic distress in the community. Instead, they chose to cut back on services.

I was busily trying to cope with the stress, anxiety, and fear that overwhelmed me during this time, and as a result I began to listen to inspirational speakers. My favorite author and speaker was Dr. Wayne Dyer. He kept me sane during those times. He helped me be strong and courageous and hold my head up high even when I felt small and scared. But his most critical advice was to practice daily meditation.

I had heard of meditation but thought it was for Buddhists, Hindus, and other Eastern religions. I didn't know how to meditate, and I didn't know how to learn, so I got on the web and began to look for resources. I found a Buddhist temple in Phoenix called the Clear Light and began attending their meditation sessions. As always, Sierra was both supportive and inquisitive. Not someone to be left out, she decided to come with me. She was somewhat familiar with Buddhism from China and was thrilled to participate and learn to meditate.

The first time we attended a session, Sierra had an unexpected reaction.

"Mom," she said, frowning as we entered the temple and saw their statue, "This is not Buddha – not *my* Buddha. Who is this guy?"

Sierra doesn't have a quiet voice even when she's not upset, and now in her distress, her words carried throughout the hushed rooms. I explained that there had been several Buddhas over the centuries, as Buddha's teachings spread throughout the world, and while this one was not the one she was familiar with, he was in fact a Buddha.

The Buddhism Sierra knew from childhood was Mahayana Buddhism. Practiced in most of China, this is the "Laughing Buddha" – usually depicted as fat and jolly – that Sierra was familiar with. The Clear Light Temple, on the other hand, displayed the Theravada Buddha – slim, serene, and serious – from India and Nepal. Sierra was disturbed that this Buddha was not the one from her memory, but she quieted down and tried to reserve judgment. We sat in the silence, observing the rituals being practiced around us to the best of our ability, and decided to keep going to the sessions.

We were joined in these meditations by two friends of mine from the County, Eric and Kimberly, who were undergoing the same stress at work. During one session, as the four of us sat in silence, we heard a man near us breathing hard. Of course, breath is an essential component of meditation, so at first, I thought nothing of it. But his breath became heavier and heavier, and slower and slower … and gradually turned into snoring. It was then I realized meditation has an amazing ability to calm the nervous system and release anxiety and stress. We all felt bad for the poor slug who snored through the session, and laughed about it after the class, but part of me thought he was the wise one, having already mastered the art of relaxation.

For many weeks, the four of us attended these training sessions. There was chanting, silent time, and prayers to Buddha. It was strange to me, but I learned to sit and watch and listen, studying the techniques they demonstrated. I began to get the hang of meditation and started to make time for it every day. This launched a regular meditation practice for me and Sierra. Today, I am a certified meditation and mindfulness instructor, but it all began with Sierra at the Buddhist temple and the Buddha who was "not her Buddha."

# Chapter 35: College, Work, and Lessons

Sierra

After graduating from high school, Sierra decided to attend Chandler/Gilbert Community College (CGCC) and work toward an associate degree. She knew she loved working with kids, so she chose to major in education. Her plan was to go to community college for two years, then transfer to Northern Arizona University (NAU) where her CGCC credits would be accepted toward a bachelor's degree in education. This is what she would need if she wanted to become a classroom teacher.

She quickly realized that college was much harder than high school. Classes were longer, her teachers were short on patience, and she began to worry about her ability to keep up.

Despite her outgoing nature, Sierra found it difficult to talk to her professors about her learning issues. When she did, though some were sympathetic and kind, others had no regard for her situation and were not helpful. She felt dejected and her confidence was shaken as she struggled to get even passing grades in her classes. She often came home from school with a long face, exhausted and irritable.

"I just don't know if I can make this work," she said one day. "I can't seem to understand the course material and I need help, but I don't feel like anyone is in my corner at this school."

In addition to driving fourteen miles each way to CGCC and trying to do homework she didn't understand, she was also still working at SJB. Her life had become hectic and stressful, and she decided she didn't like college. Because she was a freshman, she was taking a lot of general subjects that weren't related to her major, and she found them both frustrating and boring.

Meanwhile, Sedona had entered high school. Sedona had always been a smart and studious girl, and now was taking honors classes, getting straight A's. Although she was proud of her sister, this made Sierra's experience at school even more maddening. She saw Sedona flourishing in the academic setting, while she kept struggling to just pass. Sedona was now a teen herself, involved in her own school-related dramas, and she didn't spend much time with her sister. They had different passions and were on very different paths. The divide between them had widened.

PJ was in middle school and growing up fast. Sierra and PJ were eight years apart, so at this point in their lives, even though they didn't have much in common, they still got along well. Sierra worked at SJB, where PJ was still a student, so they saw a lot of each other before and after school. PJ liked having his big sister at the school and on campus. Sierra was very popular with the school administrators, teachers, and students, and PJ was proud to be associated with her. In fact, he used his sister's popularity during a student council election in seventh grade. PJ was running for Spirit Commissioner, and he was required to prepare a video to show to the entire school. He included his sister in the video and won the election.

As Sierra got further into the education program at CGCC, she found that the classes in her major didn't interest her any more than the general courses had.

*This can't be good,*" she thought.

She tried to think about how she might be able to change her major but still work with kids. Maybe she could be a school counselor? But finally she realized it wasn't the subject matter, it was college she didn't like, so in January 2015, Sierra withdrew from CGCC.

Instead, she took on more hours at SJB, working as much as she could. She threw herself into her job and her commitment to the children, working in the morning, during the lunch period, and after school. It seemed she was always on campus. She also worked special occasions, such as open houses and school fundraising events. It was at one of these events, later in 2015, that Sierra revived a talent she hadn't used since her time at the orphanage.

The school was having a parent-teacher fundraising breakfast. It was Catholic School Week, and this special event was eagerly anticipated by the entire school. Sierra was invited, as an alumna, to talk about her experience at SJB. The room was packed with parents, teachers, and administrators, and smelled of pancakes, sausage, bacon, orange juice, and coffee. The multipurpose room had over two hundred people sitting at round tables, covered with white tablecloths that were supposed to create a feeling of elegance, the ambience somewhat diminished by the paper plates and plastic silverware at every setting. But everyone was having a good time, chatting and laughing and generally enjoying each other.

The program started with an introduction by the principal and then a prayer led by the pastor of St. Benedict's. Everyone became silent and stood up, hands folded. A sense of respect and calm came over the room, like a blanket of pure white tranquility had been laid over the crowd. After the prayer, Sierra was the first official speaker. She'd been asked to talk about how SJB had changed her life when she'd attended, and she'd spent a lot of time preparing for the talk – she even had index cards with notes. But when the time came to get up and speak, she left the cards on the table and spoke from her heart.

She was so small, she couldn't stand behind the podium and be seen, so she made a joke about her height and came out onto the floor. As she spoke, she walked around the room, looking into the eyes of the audience as she connected with them. She talked about her life at the orphanage, her coming to America, and the acceptance that she had received at this incredible school. Sierra gave thanks to God, to her teachers, and to her family. She told everyone how blessed she was, and that SJB was one of her greatest blessings. "I love this school," she said. "It has taught me about tolerance, friendship, and love." When she sat down, the room thundered with applause, and many people cried silently, tears running down their faces. She was loved by this school and she had given that love back during her talk.

Just like at the orphanage in Benxi, the checkbooks came out after that.

Sierra became a school legend. Parents wanted her to watch their kids, and teachers wanted her to assist in their classrooms. A local news station even came to the school to do a story about her life and her strong tie to the school.

Unfortunately, no matter how beloved she was, she wouldn't be able to advance her career without an education degree. But despite this reality, Sierra remained optimistic. She knew that the new school administration had big plans for changes, and she believed she could be part of those plans.

# Chapter 36: Becoming

## Sierra

In the spring of 2014, many parents of Sierra's SJB students were going through divorce or other emotional upheavals in their lives, and despite her youth, she was a great source of comfort for them because of her positive attitude. She professed living moment to moment, acting with courage, and being proud of who you were – advice that serves well in most situations, no matter what your age.

But deep-down Sierra was in great pain herself.

She tried to ignore the sorrow she was feeling, tried to stay upbeat, but it was like spreading a layer of superficial joy over a dull, persistent ache. Her parents noticed the change and tried to talk with her about it.

"Are you okay?" her mom asked.

"Of course," Sierra said. "I'm just tired."

But she knew it was more than being worn out. It was something so deep that she didn't want to admit it, even to herself. It was at this point that she decided to take time off to see if she could sort through her feelings. She would go on a soul-searching expedition, a journey for reflection and contemplation.

She decided to go to Sedona, the city her sister had been named after. It was the most serene and beautiful place she could think of and she loved walking the trails, hiking up the mountains, and being surrounded by the peaceful red rocks. When she arrived, the town was bustling with tourists, the weather was perfect, and nature was putting on a show as Sedona's high desert came to life with cooler weather. The prickly pear cacti bloomed fluorescent pink, and the cottonwood trees sprouted beautiful, delicate, parakeet-green leaves. The birds were ready to return to their winter excursions southward and greeted each other with their songs. There was perfection in the natural surroundings and it brought harmony and calm to her spirit.

Sierra's family had purchased a home in Sedona as a refuge and retreat, since it was a special place for all of them. It was then they met Gary and Dale, a couple who lived two doors down from the Wilsons' new home. Gary and Dale were generous, funny, and seemed to have a lot in common with them. When the Wilsons were in town, or Gary and Dale were in Phoenix, they saw movies together, had BBQs and dinners, and even went on vacation together. It was like the two families became one.

Gary and Dale were another reason Sierra had chosen Sedona for her refuge. She had decided to confide in Gary. Gary would understand and be able to help her figure things out.

Never one to beat about the bush, she came right out and asked him, "How do you know if you're gay? I feel like I might be, but I'm not sure."

Gary and Sierra talked about it for quite a while. He offered support and asked her questions to help her get to an answer. He told her it was a very personal voyage and that only she could determine her sexual preference, but he admitted he'd had his own suspicions.

"I thought you were going to come out to me in December when we went shopping together at Christmastime. I was surprised when you didn't," he said. "But only you know the answer. Only you know the right path for yourself."

"One of the things I'm worried about is the reaction of family and friends," Sierra said, her face clouded.

"I think you know your family is very accepting" Gary said. "They'll support you, I'm sure of it. And you'll feel free once it's out and everyone knows. But don't move forward unless you've really thought about it and decided for yourself. If you feel you are gay, know that some people probably won't understand, but those are people you shouldn't have in your life. You need to surround yourself with accepting people. It's the key to happiness." He smiled.

After the conversation with Gary, Sierra searched her thoughts and feelings about her sexual orientation intensely. She had known for a long time that she was attracted to women and not men, but she had denied it for years. She had tried to have crushes on boys; it never took. She had tried to be "normal," whatever that meant, but the pain had become too great and the lies too deep. A disingenuous person was masquerading as Sierra, and it felt horribly wrong.

She told others to be themselves, but she wasn't being *her*self.

Now that she could admit the truth to herself, she considered the reaction she might get if she announced she was gay. Her mom had a government job with a lot of responsibility. Sierra knew her mom was respected at work and viewed as having a great life with a beautiful family. How would her mom's bosses view this revelation? She didn't want this to be an issue for her mom's career.

Her Catholic identity was another deep concern. She was working at a Catholic school, and the Catholic Church was certainly not supportive of this alternative lifestyle. If she stayed at SJB, she would have to live with two faces, and one of those faces would be dishonest. That would go against everything she believed in, and it would be hell. However, if she wanted to stay at SJB, it would be necessary.

Finally, Sierra made the decision: she was coming out.

But that raised more questions, and she was terrified of being rejected by the people she loved. She talked with Gary again about it, and he encouraged her to be courageous and speak her truth. He explained that he had gone through it, survived, and was thriving in a great relationship with a wonderful man. He also told her that anyone who was worth having in her life would embrace her, love her, and accept her for the beautiful person she was.

The first person she told was her mom. Sierra was with her mom in Sedona, and the rest of the family was back in Phoenix. She was petrified, even though she had a feeling her mom would understand, and she sobbed and talked at the same time. As she talked with her mom, Sierra felt like she was looking down on herself from above, observing the event disconnected from her body. Once her mom understood what she was telling her, they embraced, and Sierra's relief was immediate. Her mom comprehended the situation, and she was happy for her because she knew how important it was to Sierra that she be true to herself. Her mom would be her champion.

Sierra was afraid to tell her dad directly and asked her mom to talk with him first. After her mom broke the news to her husband, he called and had a discussion with Sierra. He said that he loved her and accepted her fully for who she truly was. Then they talked about the fact that sometimes he would make comments that might appear to be prejudiced, but that he was just trying to be funny. He knew this might have offended her in the past, and he certainly didn't want Sierra to feel misunderstood or hurt, so he would be more sensitive in the future.

Sierra also asked her mom to talk with Sedona, which she did. Sedona promptly texted her sister to give her love and support. Sierra was very touched by her sister's response, and immediately took the texts to show her mom. Later, Sedona told Sierra she wasn't surprised at her the pronouncement, that she had suspected it for a long time. Though they'd grown apart during high school, Sedona was especially attentive to her sister during this time and constantly reassured her that she loved her and would be there for her.

Finally, Sierra approached PJ. At the time, PJ was fourteen years old and in middle school. Sierra went into the room where PJ was playing his Xbox and asked if he would meet her in the kitchen so she could talk with him about something important. When PJ sat down at the kitchen table, he was surprised to see his big sister was crying. He rarely saw her sad and he was alarmed and a bit afraid, wondering if something terrible had happened to someone in the family. She began in much the same way she had with her mother, talking through her tears and not always comprehensible. Once PJ understood her, he simply got up, hugged his sister hard and said, "It's okay. I love you. It's fine. It's okay, Sierra." His face showed no condemnation, just brotherly love.

Sierra exhaled a deep sigh of relief. The immediate family had been told and the world hadn't ended.

One of the people Sierra told early on was her hair stylist, Heidi. Heidi had become a friend and confidante, and the two loved to text and talk on the phone. Sierra was sure Heidi would be supportive, so she opened her text with, "I have something important to tell you."

Heidi texted back with a simple statement. "You're gay. I've known for a long time and it's no big deal. I'm glad you're coming out because I want you to be happy."

Other friends and family were told over the next several years, and it was always a struggle for Sierra. It seemed to her that there were so many people she had to tell, and they were all so different in their personalities and beliefs that eventually someone was bound to react badly to her announcement. But it just never happened. Her aunts and uncles, cousins, extended family, and friends were all supportive. There were a few Catholic acquaintances whose approval was half-hearted, which was disappointing but not unexpected. Everyone else understood and accepted her for who she was. Her grandmother, who suffered from dementia and Alzheimer's, was the only family member who wasn't told. It was agreed that she likely wouldn't remember anyway.

Sierra has dated since her "coming out" revelation and it has resulted in a reassurance that this is what is right for her. She finally feels good in her own skin and happy about her decision to share herself completely with family and friends.

## Chapter 37:
# My Daughter's New View

Sandi

Sierra has always been an outgoing and happy individual. She's just one of those people who loves life. She's grateful and appreciative of her blessings and likes to share her positive thinking and energy with others. So when she began to be uncharacteristically depressed, I was really concerned. I tried to talk to her about it, but she was tight-lipped and shut down whenever I asked her what was wrong. This was unusual, as we had a great relationship and shared many things with each other. Paul and I talked about it, but neither one of us knew what to make of it. She was spiraling downward, and we seemed powerless to help.

I noticed the change at the end of 2013. Sierra's favorite month of the year has always been December because of Christmas. She normally started early, barely after Thanksgiving, singing Christmas songs, hanging up decorations, shopping for friends and family, and baking Christmas treats. It was family time, and we always tried to spend weekends together getting ready for the big event. But her enthusiasm for the holiday season was seriously diminished that year, and instead of singing and dancing, she was reserved and quiet. While she tried to hide it, Paul and I knew something was wrong. Yet every time we'd ask, she'd say she was fine.

This uncharacteristic behavior worsened through the end of the year. She was upbeat and cheerful one minute, and the next thing I knew, she was miserable again. She was on an elevator to the top of the skyscraper, and then she'd fall through the shaft and crash into the basement. It was like the Disneyland ride that went up to the top floor, opened to see the daylight, and then dropped to the bottom of the shaft. It was frightening to watch.

She was drinking excessively. She wasn't spending time with her family, and the weekends became a time for partying. I surmised that she was trying to drown her pain in alcohol. She'd go out with her friends and come home drunk. She slept well into the day and got up feeling hungover and nasty. It was an ugly time for Sierra, and totally unlike her. Paul and I became increasingly concerned.

In the summer of 2014, the family went to Hawaii with our friends Gary, Dale, and Kimberly. Sierra loved Hawaii, but she seemed uncomfortable being around us. Each night after dinner, she'd leave the room and go wandering. We'd find her on the beach, playing with little kids and talking with their parents, as if she was trying to insert herself into a new family rather than spend time with us. Or, if we were doing something like watching a movie on the lawn, she'd stay for a while then take off again. When I tried to get her to tell me what was wrong, she'd just say we were boring. For Sierra, who had always treasured her family, it was odd behavior.

Finally, that fall it became clear and in retrospect, it made sense: Sierra was trying to figure out her life, and one of its most elemental components, her sexuality.

Sierra finally relayed her concerns and the outcome was a great relief. She was crying, she was shaking, she sounded hopeless. Frankly, when she started talking, I couldn't understand her. Her voice didn't sound like her own. She appeared to have been possessed by an alien who was fearful and dark. I was afraid that she had gotten into an accident and hurt someone, or was on drugs, or had been arrested. The way she was carrying on, I was scared to death. When she was finally out with it and I understood what she was saying – "I'm gay" – I was relieved.

"Thank the Lord," I said. "I thought something terrible had happened!"

The relief on her face was like the sun coming out after a long, bleak winter.

It was easy for me to accept her. It just didn't make any difference to me: she was my Sierra whom I loved completely. Why she was scared that I wouldn't accept her, I'll never know – but that's what fear does to us. After we talked, I was still worried about her. I could see she was terrified that this would change her life and the people in it. I tried to tell her that her dad, Sedona, PJ, uncles and aunts and cousins and family friends, all the people who truly loved her, would be cool. But she was petrified.

She spent the next couple of years in the "coming out" phase of her life, a difficult process I did my best to help her with. When she talked with someone, she would come back and tell me their reaction. Many times she would need a lot of reassurance, and it felt like we were constantly rebuilding her self-confidence: she went into each discussion with her head high, but if it didn't go well she'd return in pieces, and we'd have to build up her faith in herself all over again. In reality, only a few friends pulled back, and she was able to see that those "friends" weren't worth worrying about. If they weren't supportive, they weren't friends.

We discussed the impact this revolution might have on her job at SJB, in light of the Catholic Church's view on homosexuality. The Church was such a big part of our lives, but I couldn't justify their attitude on this, and it began to affect my participation in parish activities and attendance. My faith was shaken, and so was Sierra's. How could the Church take a position that alienated so many beautiful, loving, and faithful people? I assured Sierra that God loved her as he built her, as she was.

Now finally, she was free to be her true self.

# Chapter 38:
# Disaster Strikes

## Sandi

The end of 2016 was a time of emotional turmoil for our family. Our lives were disrupted, and we were tested emotionally, physically, and spiritually.

It began when my elderly mother fell and broke her arm in late October. She was ninety-two years old and fragile, and as I've mentioned, suffering from dementia and Alzheimer's.

When my sister-in-law, Sheree, found her, Mom's arm had swelled, and she couldn't get out of bed. Sheree called me at the office, and we took her to the emergency room. The doctors checked her into the hospital, but because of my mother's dementia, this relatively straightforward experience was terribly traumatic. She didn't know where she was or what was happening, and she was frightened every day. After over a week in the hospital, she was released to a rehabilitation center as she needed physical therapy before she could return home.

The day she moved into rehab was surreal. The center was having a Halloween party in the parking lot and the residents were handing out candy and mingling with their families. It was loud. There was spooky music playing, a haunted house for the kids, and little goblins, witches, superheroes, and princesses milled around, chattering and laughing. This circus-like environment caused my poor mom even more consternation. And it didn't get better as the days went by.

I was working and unable to be with her all the time. I heard from the staff that she dozed a lot throughout the day, and that every time she would wake up, she'd become upset all over again because she couldn't recall what had happened or where she was. It was awful for both of us.

In early November, my work life began to deteriorate as well. I'd been working under a new boss since June, and I felt rejected, unappreciated, and exhausted. I had been a celebrated member of the management team, but those days were over. The new boss and new board members had different ideas and wanted new blood – understandable, but still hurtful for me after more than two decades with the County. Following one tense and unpleasant exchange with my boss, I decided to go out on family medical leave in November to be with my mom during her recovery. It turned out to be the absolute best thing for our family and for my mother: in

December, she came home with us to continue her recovery, and at the end of the year, I retired from Maricopa County.

Sedona was also struggling at school, not academically, but with the direction of her life. She was attending Northern Arizona University, in Flagstaff. "Flag," as it's affectionately known to Arizonans, is 150 miles north of Phoenix, nestled in a beautiful pine forest. At the time, Sedona was majoring in psychology, but had already changed her major once. She didn't like her psych classes, though she still carried a 4.0 grade point average. Our younger daughter is very bright and driven, but despite her academic success she was disappointed with college. Part of her unhappiness had to do with her living situation. She'd been unable to secure housing on campus for her sophomore year, so she was living in Munds Park, a small community south of Flagstaff, and it wasn't a great fit for her. During the Fall semester, I talked to Sedona daily about her future, her desires, her passions. It was very stressful for her and for our entire family. In the end, Sedona decided to return to Phoenix to help with her Grandmother's overnight care, leaving behind Flagstaff and determined to move in a new direction. She would attend Scottsdale Community College and major in interior design, which was a completely different focus for her life. Sedona's return to Phoenix to assist with my mom's recover was a blessing.

In early December, Sierra was rear-ended in her car while stopped at a traffic light. This was a new experience for her, and she was ill-prepared to deal with it. Being the trusting person that she was, she didn't call the cops, even though it happened on a city street. As time passed, she developed severe back pain, which became another source of worry for her and for us.

Then, in mid-December, PJ had an accident. He was playing competitive sports for the first time in high school and was on the JV soccer team. He came home one night after practice with his leg in a brace after he had collided with another player during a scrimmage. He was clearly in agony, his face drawn, and his normally calm, cheerful demeanor scrambled like a puzzle. I took him to the emergency room, where they determined he had a broken leg. It was the second time he had broken a bone playing soccer; when he was in grade school, he had broken his ankle in a match. Soccer was one of PJ's favorite things in life, but the sport seemed to be a physical disaster for him. For the rest of the month, he was stuck in his bedroom. He missed his final exams, didn't get to enjoy his school break, and had a very boring Christmas.

The final blow occurred on Christmas day. All the bedrooms in our house are upstairs, but because of my mom's immobility, we had made her a bedroom downstairs in what had been the family room. That day we were celebrating at home with my brother, Bob, and his family, as well as Mom and our three kids. Everyone was having a wonderful time – good food, good company, and good conversation.

Then PJ came out of the bathroom and said, "The toilet is overflowing in the downstairs bathroom."

We had just had the plumber out a couple of weeks before to deal with this same problem. He had snaked the pipe, and the issue had seemed resolved. But now the problem was not only back, but it was affecting all the toilets in the house. We called the plumber, but the cost for coming out on the holiday was $300 – and that was just for the service call. There would be additional costs on top of that. This persuaded us to wait until the next day to have the issue fixed, and Christmas was cut short as Bob and his family headed home.

The plan for the Wilsons' evening was to avoid flushing any toilets. We could use them, but not flush. We could also go next door to our neighbors, but that was a pain. The plumber was scheduled to come out at 8:00 a.m. the next day, and we figured we could survive the putrid situation that long. We didn't realize there was one little detail we'd forgotten.

The next morning, most of the downstairs was flooded. During the night the soft-water system had gone through its clearing cycle and overflowed the toilet and shower, then flooded the entire bathroom with two inches of water, which spilled out into the hallway, laundry room, and family room. The carpet was drenched, the built-in cabinets were saturated, and even the walls were soaked.

My mom woke up to a waterlogged mess in her room, and I realized she couldn't stay with us while the house was in this state – her health was too precarious. After talking to my brother Bob, he agreed to take her in the short term, and we decided to get 24/7 home care for her, which her doctors had said was the best thing for her Alzheimer's condition. Once Mom was securely moved, we still had to deal with the aftermath of the flooding, but at least I knew she was safe.

I felt like I was playing cards with the Universe and it was dealing me nothing but jokers. I was angry and worn out, and could only hope that 2017 would bring better luck.

## Chapter 39:
# Pain and Sorrow

### Sierra

December 2, 2016. Sierra was on her way to see Heidi to get her hair done. She was in good spirits and looking forward to the holiday season, pleased that Christmas was on its way. It was her special time of year. But that day, as she sat waiting for a red light to change, she was suddenly jolted forward with a terrific crash.

Sierra climbed out of the car upset and confused, to see a Mercedes-Benz sedan had plowed into the rear of her car. She was disoriented, shaking, and half-crying. Once the fog began to clear, she recognized the face of man who hit her.

"Sir, haven't I seen you on TV?"

"I work for the Arizona Cardinals," he said.

Sierra didn't call the cops because she didn't know that she should, but she did know to exchange insurance information. Her car was damaged but drivable, so she left the scene and continued on her way. When she got to Heidi's, she was anxious about what had happened and worried about her car. When she told Heidi the name of the man who hit her, Heidi told her he was a senior manager of the Arizona Cardinals and that he made millions of dollars each year. This made Sierra feel a little better because she thought such a man would certainly be responsible.

In the next couple of days, her car was brought into the auto repair shop and when it was fixed it looked good as new. Unfortunately, the same couldn't be said for Sierra, who had begun to experience pain shortly after the accident and had gone to the emergency room the same day to get it checked out. They didn't find any problems, but it wasn't long before she was in constant and excruciating pain.

So began a cycle of ER visits, doctor appointments, X-rays, MRIs, and tests. She saw primary care doctors, urgent care doctors, emergency doctors, and pain and back specialists. As a result, her life changed dramatically. She was unable to exercise, hike or walk, or participate in any physical activity. Going to the mall or even standing for more than a few minutes was agonizing. She was also on heavy pain medication, so her pastimes became sleeping and lying around watching TV.

Unable to be her usual active self, and in pain despite the meds, depression settled like fog over her days. She hated the change in herself. After everything she'd been through, she knew the way to survive what life threw at you was to be joyful and optimistic, yet at this point she felt anything but. When she looked at herself in the mirror, the reflection that stared back at her was a stranger. This morose, exhausted person wasn't who she wanted to be, but the pain clouded everything, and her energy was nonexistent. Sierra just wanted to climb into a box, close the top, and curl into a ball in the dark, where she could sleep and be forgotten. This lasted for several months.

In addition, she found that the insurance company handling the accident claim for the individual who'd hit her wouldn't pay her medical bills, so she decided to hire an attorney to help her get reimbursed for medical costs. This was an additional layer of stress she didn't need, and in the meantime, she still had to come up with out-of-pocket money for co-pays, expensive prescriptions, ER visits, and doctor's appointments. Sierra didn't have this kind of money, and she was constantly receiving collection calls for these unexpected medical costs.

Then, as spring began, Sierra met Julianna. Julianna was a beautiful young Brazilian woman living in Phoenix who had reached out to her on a dating website. It wasn't long before they were constantly texting and chatting on the phone. They appeared to have a lot in common, and Sierra was lovestruck. The two met and hit it off right away. Julianna was petite, with a fresh face, brunette hair, and piercing brown eyes. She had an engaging, fun personality, which was just what Sierra needed. The two became inseparable. They went to the movies, hung out, ate meals, and were introduced to each other's families.

Sierra wasn't completely herself during these months because despite her joy at meeting Julianna she was still in pain. This meant that she was often short-tempered and always tired, which created problems for them as a couple. Juliana was an active, happy girl, and Sierra couldn't keep up with her or participate in activities she enjoyed. After a couple of months, Juliana called a halt to their relationship.

This left Sierra with a broken heart and nothing to divert her from the intense back pain. Her depression intensified. The pain became the focus of her life. She thought and talked about it constantly and felt it grow more severe every day.

Going to work became increasingly difficult but she pushed on. She lived for the distraction of the children, which gave her a purpose beyond her injury. But when she came home in the evenings, she was spent, exhausted physically and emotionally. She'd retreat to her room and hide away from everyone.

The only bright spot during this dark time was her ukulele. PJ had learned to play the four-stringed instrument several years earlier, and Sierra decided to teach herself how to play after taking a class during a trip to Hawaii. The ukulele has a sweet, tranquil sound, and Sierra took to it immediately. She spent time on the Internet learning new songs and she became quite an adept player. Whenever she strummed the ukulele, her mood lightened a bit.

Sierra gave up her job at St. John Bosco in May of 2017. Standing and running after the kids was taking a huge toll on her back, to the point she couldn't enjoy her work. While her back issues hadn't caused her pain prior to the accident, doctors believed her natural spinal fusion exacerbated the injuries she received in the crash, and now the incessant pain was another brick in the wall of her depression.

The darkness was always there. The broken heart mixed with her back pain formed a cord of despair that coiled and tightened around her, suffocating her spirit, like a python constricting on prey. Her mental, physical, and emotional health continued to deteriorate, and her parents became more and more alarmed.

One evening Sierra was talking on the phone in her room when a knock came on the door. "Honey, are you okay?" It was her mother's voice.

Sierra opened the door. Her mother said, "Your eyes are red, have you been crying? Who were you talking to?"

"I was talking to the suicide hotline," Sierra said. "I feel like I'm done, Mom. This pain is just too intense, and I need it to stop," she said through sobs.

Her mom was dumbfounded, but being a problem-solver, quickly became relentless about having her daughter see a psychologist. She found several close to home and pestered Sierra until she reluctantly picked one, a woman in her thirties.

Her mother went with her to several sessions until she became comfortable with the psychologist. It didn't take long before Sierra began to relax and feel better after her appointments. The doctor didn't just help with her depression but taught her how to deal with the physical pain so it didn't rule her life. She began to find her stability and peace of mind.

The real Sierra began to reemerge and her life again began to shine.

# Chapter 40:
# Help Me, Please

### Sandi

The aftermath of the Great Toilet Flood of 2016 was the backdrop for the first six months of 2017. The insurance adjuster came out and determined that the flooring downstairs needed to be replaced, as did the shower and vanity in the guest bathroom; the built-in cabinets needed to be refurbished; and many downstairs walls needed to be torn out and replaced. In other words, our home was to become a construction zone once again.

Before anything else could happen, we had to get rid of all the excess moisture. The sound of the huge industrial fans whooshed and howled in our house for a week, making a deafening noise as we dried out the carpet, the walls, and the cabinets. It was impossible to think during this phase. I remember my head pounding like a big bass drum whenever I entered the space. And the smell was plain nasty. Even in dry Arizona, the mold had been quick to colonize, and it smelled like dirty gym socks had been left all over the house. The furniture had been moved every which way, looking like a tornado had touched down inside. You could feel the black cloud of negativity the minute you stepped in the door.

Meanwhile, Sierra's pain was becoming intolerable. Working at SJB with the kids was her only relief, her only distraction. Much of the time she was unable to work because her job required her to stand for long periods, which she couldn't do with her back in such agony. It's the only time I ever remember seeing Sierra as completely fragile. My vibrant, vivacious girl was feeble, depressed, and weak, and her mood was gloomy.

She would lie down on the floor and I would lean on her, putting pressure on her back. It was one of the few things that gave her any relief. She'd come home from work and immediately go to bed. No more working out in the evening. No more going out with friends.

One day, Sedona came home from school and wanted to have a girls' day – go to the mall and shop, eat lunch together, and maybe take in a movie. This was something all three of us loved. Sedona approached her sister, thinking a day out would lift her spirits and distract her from the pain.

But Sierra only snapped, "Sedona, I can't go to the mall! Do you have any idea how much pain I'm in? I can't do anything but lie in bed and watch TV. I don't know if I'll ever be able to do normal things again."

Sedona was usually quiet, remote, and low-key, but this time, she found herself playing the optimist. Sierra just couldn't see the sun as she was perpetually stuck in the shadow.

Sierra had a brief period of happiness when she met Juliana and began a relationship with her. Both girls were petite and pretty, and they made a striking couple. The family got to know Juliana, and we all thought she was terrific. However, their relationship burned out quickly, and this left Sierra even more distressed.

Sierra went to doctor after doctor for relief; they put her on opioids and other pain medications, which dulled the constant agony, but didn't alleviate it completely. The opioids made her emotional state even more tenuous and it became clear she needed to avoid those drugs.

She had been to the emergency room three times in Phoenix. Then, one weekend, when we were at our getaway in Sedona, Sierra's pain reached a critical point. We called our friend Dale, who was an emergency room doctor in Sedona. He asked us to meet him at the ER so he could treat her. He administered morphine and put her under observation, then gave her a numbing patch of lidocaine. The change after he applied the topical anesthetic patch was miraculous. Apparently, lidocaine was exactly what she'd needed all along. The doctors in Phoenix were unable to think beyond dangerous, addictive painkillers, yet this much gentler method actually *helped*. Sierra stopped using the opioids immediately.

The lidocaine gave her the ability to function physically, but her emotional state was still extremely delicate, and she remained depressed. She cried. She slept. She wouldn't eat. She lost ten pounds in a couple of months – which may not sound like a lot, but considering her small size, it was more than 10 percent of her total body weight. She isolated herself from friends and family. This gregarious, outgoing, larger-than-life young woman was becoming a glum recluse.

While all this was going on, things at SJB were also changing. At this point, Sierra had been working for the school for eight years. Many of the original teachers who were there when the school began had been let go the year before, perhaps in an effort to lower the payroll by bringing in less-experienced and lower-paid teachers. There was a new principal and many new faces at the school. Sierra was unhappy. Many of her "adult" friends were no longer there, and she felt that her worth had diminished in the eyes of the administration. The families still loved her and gave her compliments daily, but her boss and the principal didn't appear to value her, and in her frame of mind she worried that she'd done something to earn their displeasure. She decided this was going to be her last year at SJB.

With three weeks left in the school year, she went to the principal and explained she was giving her notice.

"I love SJB," she said, "but I need to find my calling and move on in my life." Sierra went on to tell her that she felt that her position had been devalued and that she needed a bigger challenge.

Before she could finish, the principal piped in. "Sierra, I want you to leave today," she said. "No need to stay and complete the school year. We can manage without you. I'll have someone escort you to get your things."

Sierra looked at her, stunned. "You're going to have me walked off of campus?"

"Yes."

Sierra was horrified. She wondered what she had done to deserve this treatment. She had been a good and loyal employee for almost a decade. She had brought positive energy and joy to the school and had given them everything she had to give. She couldn't believe what she was hearing.

"I can't say goodbye to the kids?" she asked.

"I think it's best that you just leave. We'll pay you through the end of the school year. This will give you an opportunity to look for another job."

Sierra was crushed. She had loved this school and everyone in it, and had felt loved in return. Now she was being told to leave without being able to say goodbye or thank those who had been so good to her over the years. This wasn't how she wanted to leave, and it was a dismal end to a wonderful chapter of her life.

Her departure from SJB deepened her depression and I became even more worried about her. When I was with her, she rarely wanted to talk, and I tried not to push. I would just be there with her, for her, sitting in quiet anguish. She was living her own personal nightmare. It was like I was watching a horror flick, but I couldn't understand the dialogue, so I couldn't follow the plot. While leaving my career had been traumatic for me, at that point I was glad because I knew I was meant to be home with Sierra, to provide support and to keep her from hurting herself.

One night, I overheard her talking on the phone to someone. After asking her about the call, I was shocked to find that she had called the suicide hotline. It was a huge wake-up call that she needed me to take the reins.

I convinced Sierra to go to a psychologist. Her resistance to seeking professional help was intense. She had always projected positivity and happiness, and allowing a stranger to help *her* feel better didn't fit her self-image. But after admitting to me that she was considering suicide, she agreed to go.

Her psychologist was fantastic. She taught Sierra new coping skills. Despite having learned to meditate with me, she was unable to practice it with any resolve during her depression; her psychologist gave her guided visualization meditations, and, in these meditations, Sierra was to give her pain a color, shape, and presence. Then she would let the pain drift away, like a balloon floating off into the bright, blue sky. She learned tapping techniques, where you tap with your fingers on different parts of the body to calm the nervous system. Sierra was educated in the practice of embracing her pain, loving her pain, and then letting it go and moving to those things that made her happy.

These counseling sessions made a huge difference in Sierra's mood and state of mind, and she began to turn the corner. I praised the Lord. As the hot Phoenix summer sun began to descend upon us, Sierra began to come out from the clouds again.

As her mental and physical pain began to subside, she was sent to physical therapy to strengthen her back. This was a long process of over four months of biweekly sessions. Some days it was extremely painful, but it resulted in a stronger, healthier spine, and an increased confidence that she was able to return to some of her prior physical stamina. She has continued to work independently on her back muscles and her endurance ever since, and while not completely able to meet her pre-accident vigor, she continues to improve her resilience.

# Chapter 41: A New Day

## Sandi

After emerging from her depression, Sierra started to put her life back together. She got a new job at Desert Lights Gymnastics working with kids, but in an entirely different capacity than at St. John Bosco. This was what she needed. She was hired as a coach, even though she was not a gymnast. Her first assignment was to work with toddlers through early elementary-age children, and she quickly impressed everyone with her ability to be firm and strong, but also encouraging, energetic, and light-hearted. The students took to her as children always did, and the classes Sierra taught filled up so fast the gym opened additional classes for her to teach. This gave Sierra back the confidence she'd lost during her departure from SJB.

Sierra truly loved coaching gymnastics and providing a class that was both challenging and fun. She was in awe of the children's athletic abilities and their pure determination, and loved watching them pour everything into their sessions. Desert Lights is one of the only gymnastics gyms in Arizona that has coached girls who have qualified for the Junior Olympics, so it's known as having a great program. The owners, John and Lisa Spini, were kind to Sierra. Their encouragement helped her think of new ways she could teach and encourage others.

Eventually this led to a new passion for teaching fitness, which in turn led her to pursue a professional career in personal training and coaching.

At last Sierra knew she'd found her calling.

In the Fall of 2017, Sierra began taking a course to become a certified personal trainer. She wanted to encourage and help others achieve their fitness goals and improve their health. She'd always been good at supporting others, and she knew firsthand how important a positive self-image was; she could use these skills to help her clients lead better lives physically, emotionally, and spiritually.

There was one little problem: Sierra had test phobia.

It was one of the reasons it had taken her so many tries to pass the AIMS test, and why the community college challenges had seemed insurmountable. After she left SJB, she had gone to real estate school to become an agent. Once she had completed the course, she took the test, but became discouraged when she didn't pass the first time.

She worried about passing her personal trainer exam and talked about this fear daily. But unlike other courses she'd taken in the past, she really wanted this, so she studied constantly, took notes on each chapter, and logged the theories into a notebook to help cement the concepts into her head.

She completed her coursework in eight months, and began preparing for the certification exam, which would be completed online. As Sierra continued trying to imprint the knowledge on her brain, her nervousness reached a dangerous level. I felt like if she didn't pass the exam, she would fall into a deep depression again because this was so important to her. In her mind, she was already a personal trainer.

Every day, I saw her sitting at the kitchen island, where she frequently studied, and as I walked by, I could feel the tension. It hung in the air like a ball of smoke, thick and gray. I wished there was some way to help her, but apart from providing moral support and encouragement, there was nothing I could do.

Then, one morning while I was driving, I got a call from Sierra.

"I did it, Mom! I passed the certification test!" She talked fast, laughing and screaming with joy. Though I was frustrated that she hadn't even told me she was going to take it, her elation was irresistible. It was as if there was a golden light bursting from her soul, and I was so, so proud of her. I felt tears well up in my eyes, knowing that her dreams were coming true. She was going to be a personal trainer and it was a beautiful day.

Shortly after she passed her test, Sierra began a video series she called "Weekly Words of Wisdom." Every Monday, she put together a video about a topic like forgiveness, self-love, mindfulness, kindness, life's purpose, or respect, to name a few, and posted it on Facebook and Instagram. These videos were very popular with her friends, family and coworkers, and were often shared and passed on to those who needed them. It was yet another way for Sierra to be of service to others.

Sierra's court case on the accident in 2016 continued for three years. It was dreadful that she had to relive the emotional turmoil and physical pain. There were depositions taken, derogatories to review, and lengthy discussions with her attorney. Sierra's demands were minimal, as she only wanted the insurance company to pay for her medical bills – she wasn't looking for a financial windfall. Because of the dollar amount of the claim, the superior court judge sent the case to binding arbitration. Sierra was scrutinized and grilled, while the person who caused the accident didn't even have to appear. It was a difficult day, and in the end, Sierra was only minimally compensated. If it hadn't been for her legal staff, she wouldn't have been able to even pay off the medical bills. But her legal team worked with the medical providers and they settled for less than the full amount of her outstanding bills. The Arizona Cardinals' manager, who was arrested for extreme DUI after the accident and before the arbitration, walked away without any additional liability, or any apparent repercussions. Despite the turmoil, pain, and expense the accident had caused, Sierra took the outcome in stride and was grateful to her law firm for helping her get out of debt.

On the other hand, I felt that the legal system had failed my daughter and put her through additional suffering. Sierra saw the glass half full. God bless her optimism.

My beautiful girl is only a little over a quarter of a century old, but wise beyond her age. She's an old soul sent to inspire, offer advice, be a friend, and remind everyone to have fun. Her happiness is contagious. She's learned to forgive those who have wronged her, to move past those who have bullied her. While she enjoys being with others, Sierra now understands that joy and contentment can come in the silence of our hearts, when we are alone. She has had her heart broken but has moved on to be a spiritual being filled with acceptance for others even when it doesn't align with her wishes.

"I'm in a happy place," Sierra told me recently. "I know what it means to be fulfilled. It's not about material possessions. It's not about what others think. It's about being yourself, the person you are deep within your soul. Through meditation, thankfulness, self-acceptance, and forgiveness, we can all find peace."

Despite Sierra's difficult beginning, she has become an inspiration and a mentor to many. Her actions, attitude, and gratitude have made her a positive force and her optimistic energy is changing the world, one person at a time.

Sierra is luck times two for everyone she meets.

# Epilogue: Adoption Challenges

Our adoption journey began in 1996. At the time, I had been off birth control for over eight years, and pregnancy had eluded us. We didn't undertake fertility treatments, but we were trying to get pregnant and were unsuccessful. In fact, we went so far as to get fertility testing, but decided that proceeding with infertility treatment was not for us.

It had all started rather suddenly. Paul and I were cruising along, happily childless as we pursued our careers, when I abruptly proclaimed that I needed a child. Most of my friends had children by then, and I was one of the only married women in my peer group who didn't. That had never bothered me in the past, but in 1996, suddenly there was a siren shrieking in my brain. I was thirty-five years old and I wanted a child. My first baby might arrive later than usual, but I was determined it would arrive. Paul and talked about it and decided it was now or never. When we didn't get pregnant ourselves, adoption seemed like a great option, and once we made the decision, we were resolute.

I began my research on the Internet, learning about domestic and international adoptions. I read books, talked to experts, called social services agencies, and prayed. There was so much to know, and at the time, I was ignorant of all of it.

I investigated domestic adoptions and found that adopting an older child in the foster care system was a possible solution. However, the best way to do that would be to become foster parents. Many times, children in the American foster system are part of a family crisis and foster care is only a temporary situation for the kids. These children have been taken from one or both parents due to physical or emotional abuse, drug use, incarceration, or neglect. If the families can put the crisis behind them, the children are reunited with their birth parents. If we became foster parents, we could become attached to the child without any certainty that an adoption was going to be possible.

Some kids in the foster care system awaited adoption because their birth parents' parental rights had been severed, but they were usually older children. Many of them had been in the foster care system for years and had gone from foster family to foster family. This sounded like another possible option, but as much as my heart broke for those kids, we wanted our first child to be a baby or toddler.

I soon discovered that domestic infant adoptions are usually handled by attorneys outside the foster care system. Birth mothers contact adoption agencies or attorneys during pregnancy and indicate that they are considering adoption for their unborn child. Then potential adoptive parents submit background paperwork to the agencies or adoption attorneys. The birth mother reviews the potential adoptive parents, meets with prospective couples, then selects a family whom she feels is appropriate for her child. The matched potential adoptive parents pay for the prenatal care, delivery, and related medical costs. After the child is born, the biological mother has up to seventy-two hours to change her mind and rescind the adoption decision. This means the adoptive parents have no assurance that the adoption will become final. If the mother reverses course, the adoptive parents are left without a child. This is not only costly, but heartbreaking. I spoke with several women who had been left at the hospital without a child when the birth mother decided to keep the baby. These women were devastated, and I didn't want to risk such an outcome.

After all my research, Paul and I decided to go the international adoption route. We knew the process could be long, but we also knew that the children were available, all parental rights were already severed, and no change in the adoption status of the child would occur.

Two countries interested us most: Russia and China. At the time, these were the most popular international adoption countries. Each had its positive and negative aspects, and each was an expensive undertaking.

We investigated Arizona international adoption agencies that were certified to complete adoptions in these two countries, and after much consideration, chose Hand-in-Hand

International Adoptions in Mesa. We truly loved the staff at this facility, and one of the selling points was that the agency offered extra services like parenting classes and a support group for waiting families. Paul and I felt like we needed all the help we could get.

Next, we had to make a definitive decision on the country of choice. We talked with the program coordinators for both countries. We decided on China because we found that the Russian program often referred children with fetal alcohol poisoning. In China, families could adopt a baby who was healthy, or a special needs baby with few issues.

In addition, China had thousands of girls awaiting a family. This was because in 1979, due to explosive population growth, China had instituted a one-child policy for couples. This led many families whose first child was a girl to give up or abort the child in the hope that their next pregnancy would produce a boy – girls being perceived as less desirable in Chinese culture. (The one-child policy changed in 2016: couples can have two children if they petition the government.)

For those considering a Chinese international adoption, the situation is different now than when we adopted in 1998 and 2004. There are still six hundred thousand orphans awaiting permanent homes in China, but most of these orphans have disabilities, like Sierra did at birth.

A decade ago, China's orphanages were filled with healthy girls, a situation that reflected a national one-child policy and a cultural preference for boys. Now Chinese authorities estimate that fully 98 per cent of abandoned children have disabilities. As the once-draconian rules limiting couples to one child are being phased out, parents are giving up these children because they simply can't afford their care in a country whose social safety nets remain poorly constructed and incomplete. (Vanderklippe)

If you're considering adopting from China, a willingness to accept a disabled child may be necessary.

Once Paul and I had settled on China for the adoption, we started filling out what seemed like endless amounts of paperwork. We had to produce certified birth certificates, our marriage license, paycheck stubs, bank statements, health status records, and our household budget. There were forms to fill out for the United States and the Chinese government. It was every bit as tedious as it sounds.

Another hurdle was the home study required for all adoptions. This is a comprehensive process that necessitates a social worker visit the home to interview the potential parents, looking at the applicants' suitability for parenthood. They ask myriad questions about all aspects of the couple's life – it can feel very invasive. They also walk through the home to assess the safety of the environment and to ensure that it has been childproofed. In our case, we needed to furnish our living room, prepare a nursery, and fence our pool.

Expenses related to adoption can be quite steep and often entail potential parents borrowing funds to complete the process. Such was the case for our three adoptions. There were government fees, adoption agency fees, travel, and the cost of ensuring our home was safe and appropriate for each child. We cut out luxuries as we saved money for the adoption costs. We also wanted to see if we could live on a budget that included day care, so we began to set aside the money we would use each month for this purpose.

After all the paperwork is finished, an adoption dossier is assembled. This involves the preparation of a wide range of legal documents necessary to obtain permission to adopt from the foreign government and must also fulfill the immigration requirements of the United States government. Once it's completed, it must be translated into the language of the adopting country – another cost to be paid by the adopting parents.

The final step is the wait. International adoption is a long and tedious road filled with potholes, hidden curves, and unexpected stops, and requires more patience than you may think you have. It's vital for the waiting parents to take care of themselves during this period, though, because once the child enters the home, there won't be any slack time. During the wait for Sedona, we took parenting classes and attended the weekly waiting parent support group. We completed the nursery, bought baby clothes and accessories (high chair, car seat, etc.) My office at Maricopa County threw a baby shower for Paul and me after we received our referral. That made the event feel fully real and I began to mentally prepare to be a mother.

It was fourteen months after we completed all the paperwork before we received a match, then it was another month before we were able to go to China to pick up Sedona. This was the longest part of the wait. It seemed like each day was forty-eight hours long. I worried like any new parent, but now that I knew Sedona would be ours, I was filled with an inner light.

As we waited, we braced ourselves for any mental or physical issues we might encounter with this new addition to our family. The parenting classes had discussed separation anxiety, attachment disorder, developmental delays, and other potential problems common with international adoptions. We faced several of these with all three of our children.

Like Sierra, many older Chinese adoptees have spent time in a boarding school while in their birth country.

It is no surprise that many of the children have psychological issues and many contemplate suicide. A study by Stanford, the University of California at Davis, the Chinese Academy of Sciences, and Catholic University of Leuven found that fourth-graders in rural areas are at least two grade levels behind their urban peers in math and Chinese. (Roberts)

Research also indicates that children in a boarding school setting average three centimeters shorter than nonboarders. This is probably because the children do not receive proper nutrition in these institutions, as we believe was the case with Sierra.

These issues can happen with biological children too, of course, but they're more prevalent in international adoptions.

A meta-analysis showed that internationally adopted children exhibit more behavioral problems and receive more mental health services than non-adopted children. Higher rates of attachment and social-emotional problems also were found among internationally adopted children when compared to non-adopted and domestically adopted peers. As such, this group needs to be considered an at-risk population deserving of specific attention. (Liu and Hazler)

However, we found that our kids, with love and consistent parenting practices, adjusted well after arriving in the United States.

Our international adoptions occurred in 1998, 2001, and 2004. Since that time, the number of international adoptions has declined significantly. International adoptions to the United States from Russia stopped due to political issues in 2012. In 2008, international adoptions in Guatemala were virtually eliminated after it was found there was significant corruption in the system. This overall decrease in international adoption leaves a void for Americans. "By 2015 international adoptions had dropped 72 percent, to 12,000 in total. Just 5,500 of these children ended up in the U.S., with the remainder landing in Italy and Spain" (The Conversation). There has been much said about abuse within the international adoption system. Identified issues include abuse of economically challenged birth mothers, child trafficking, removal of the child from his or her birth culture, and biracial issues. However, there are also studies showing that children transported to affluent countries receive a better education and achieve significant personal and professional success.

International adoption has changed my life and the lives of my family, and all for the better. We're staunch proponents for the continuation of this practice. Of course, the process should be monitored to ensure everything is legal, fair, and safe for everyone involved, but the advantages to both the adoptive parents and adoptees cannot be ignored. Most of the tens of thousands of international adoptees in the United States are happy, productive members of our society with opportunities that would not have been available to them in their birth countries – in fact, most of these adoptees wouldn't have found permanent homes if they hadn't been adopted internationally.

I understand why many people oppose international adoptions, but I'd ask everyone to consider the significant improvement in the lives of the adoptees that simply comes from living in a permanent home where the children are actively wanted. Children need the love of parents, and that love can come from outside their birth culture. International adoptions are a "win-win" for any country and certainly for the families that receive these children. Family is not defined by color, race, ethnicity, religion, or social convention.

Family is defined by love.

# Resources

## Adoption Agencies

1. **Bethany Christian Services**
   http://www.bethany.org/
2. **Hand in Hand International Adoptions**
   https://hihiadopt.org/
3. **Holt International**
   https://www.holtinternational.org/
4. **Spence-Chapin**
   https://www.spence-chapin.org/
5. **Hopscotch Adoptions**
   http://www.hopscotchadoptions.org/
6. **All God's Children International**
   https://allgodschildren.org/

## Adoption Organizations

7. **North American Council on Adoptable Children**
   970 Raymond Avenue
   Suite 106
   St. Paul, MN 55114, 651-644-3036
   info@nacac.org
8. **Child Welfare Information Gateway**
   Children's Bureau/ACYF
   330 C Street S.W.
   Washington, DC 20201, info@childwelfare.gov

# Works Cited


"International Adoptions Have Dropped 72% since 2005 – Here's Why," *The Conversation*. February 28, 2018.

Liu, YanHong, and Hazler, Richard J. "The Professional Counselor, All Foreign-Born Adoptees Are Not the Same: What Counselors and Parents Need to Know," *The Professional Counselor*. March, 2015.

Roberts, Dexter. "China's Dickensian Boarding Schools." *Bloomberg Business*. April 6, 2015. Web. July 12, 2015.

*The Guardian*, "China's Great Gender Crisis." November 2, 2011.

Vanderklippe, Nathan. "The Tragic Tale of China's Orphanages: 98% of Abandoned Children Have Disabilities." *The Globe and Mail*. Updated May 12, 2018.

Made in the USA
Las Vegas, NV
16 December 2021

38114714R00152